Principles of
KINGDOM
LIVING

"How to Live Right in a World Gone Wrong"

Dr. Darrow Perkins, Jr., Th.D.

COPYRIGHT

Principles of Kingdom Living: How to Live Right in a World Gone Wrong

Copyright © 2015 Darrow Perkins, Jr. All rights reserved. No part of this book may be reproduced or retransmitted in any form or by any means without the written permission of the publisher.

Cover image by Shawn Davis.

Published by Workin Perkins Media
P. O. Box 231271
San Diego, CA 92193

Unless otherwise noted, all Scripture quotations are taken from the King James Version of the Bible

Because of the dynamic nature of the Internet, any web addresses or links contained in this book may have changed since publication and may no longer be valid. The views expressed in this work are solely those of the author and do not necessarily reflect the views of the publisher, and the publisher hereby disclaims any responsibility for them.

Additional copies of this book can be ordered from:
www.darrowperkinsjr.com

Perkins, Darrow Jr.

Principles of Kingdom Living: How to Live Right in a World Gone Wrong / by Darrow Perkins, Jr.

ISBN: 978-1-931130-45-5

Printed in the United States of America

Dedication

This book is dedicated to my family, who have been with me throughout this journey with my Lord and Savior, Jesus Christ.

To my parents, Darrow Sr. and Lilly Perkins who were used by God to bring me into this world, exposed me to a relationship with Jesus Christ and taught me how to be a man and a productive citizen in my community.

To my wife, Teresa, who has been with me almost my entire adult life, has been there through the good times and the bad times and has loved me throughout.

To my three children, Stephanie, Tara, and Darrow III, all of whom I had the opportunity to share Christ with, and the awesome privilege of baptizing.

Acknowledgements

Having accepted Christ into my life, He used various people to help guide, mold and counsel me in my walk with the Lord. I'd like to take a few minutes to acknowledge some of them:

Pastor Charles Reynolds who saw something in me and afforded me an opportunity to work at the Mt. Olive Missionary Baptist Church in Okinawa, Japan, first as a Musician, then as a Sunday School Teacher and eventually as an Ordained Deacon;

Pastor Quintin R. Smith, Sr., of the Historical First Baptist Church of Millington, TN, who licensed and ordained me in the Gospel Ministry;

Dr. David C. Greene of the Linda Vista Second Baptist Church of San Diego, CA, for suggesting the Andersonville Theological Seminary to me that I may continue my education in order to edify God's people.

The great people of the Mesa View Baptist Church of Poway, CA. We have grown together and it's my sincere prayer that what I've shared with you by way of sermons, teaching, and conferences has made a difference in your lives.

Foreword

For more than 17 years I have had the privilege of referring to Dr. Darrow Perkins, Jr., as a friend and fellow preacher of the Gospel, and as such, the best any of us can do is direct everyone we come in contact with to the message of the cross of Jesus Christ. I am therefore excited about his very practical and thought-provoking offering, ***Principles of Kingdom Living: How To Live Right In a World Gone Wrong.***

The title alone identifies the need for there to be principles in this 21st century culture that in my estimation is quite reminiscent of the biblical Babylon. This book contains understandable biblical truths, "that will preach" and also provide the seeker and committed Christian "the how to be" a kingdom citizen in a world that's so far away from God's plan for man.

In my own experiences people are looking for answers and there is no better place to find those answers than in the Word of God. The Bible is the most important book in the world, period. When you read the Bible, you read the message from God Himself. When the Bible speaks, God speaks. Because the Bible is God's Word, it does more than just pass on information. It makes a promise, a promise of life. Everyone who receives the message of the Bible in faith is promised the gift of eternal life in the Lord Jesus Christ.

Using the Bible as the foundation for his book, every subject matter that Dr. Perkins raises up strikes the very core of our human existence and that is so much of what our soul needs. The soul is hungry for the living word and the pages of this book beckons everyone to come to the table of the Lord to be fed. This is the promise of Matthew 5:16, "Blessed are those who hunger and thirst for righteousness, for they will be filled."

Dr. Perkins, a well traveled man uses many personal experiences to explain and interpret scripture in a unique way. His honest approach to such interpretation causes one to consider his/her own experiences to help make Scripture applicable. This spirit-led book, true to scripture analysis will greatly assist in one's own understanding of God's Word and help the citizens of the Kingdom of God to live right in a world gone wrong.

Bishop Osco E. Gardin, Jr., M.Div.
Senior Pastor, Elizabeth Missionary Baptist Church
Founder/Director, United Covenant Churches International

Introduction

Bookstores today are filled with "self-help" books covering every aspect of daily life. What we sometimes tend to forget is that God put together a "how-to" book centuries ago and packaged it in what He calls the Holy Bible. This collection of 66 individual books contains the very best "how-to" guidance known to man to help us navigate our way through this race before us called life.

There has been a moral decline in our society and it is effecting how we live and operate on a daily basis. Manners have fallen by the wayside; good order and discipline is no longer the "norm;" and people have turned to do whatever they feel grown enough to do, without any thought of consequence. This, I believe, is not the way God intended, but He is longsuffering towards us as society overwhelmingly continues to do things contrary to His will and word.

In this book, I've attempted to take the basic teachings of Jesus Christ as found in His "Sermon on the Mount" and put them into a practical application for daily living.

Jesus made it a point to re-emphasize most of the Ten Commandments (minus the keeping of the Sabbath Day) and made them plain for our understanding. Since times have changed, my goal was to take the timeless principles of the Word of God and make them understandable and "do-able" for us today.

It is my sincere hope and desire that as you "peruse the periphery" of what has been proclaimed, you will find this book as both helpful and a blessing in your life.

Serving the Lord and His People,

Dr. Darrow Perkins, Jr.

Table of Contents

Going Through!	09
Thriving	15
Triumphing	23
Being A True Disciple	29
Turn On The Light!	37
Jesus And The Law	47
Get Your Righteousness Right!!	53
Get Your Relationships Right, Part I	59
Get Your Relationships Right, Part II	67
Say What You Mean, And Mean What You Say!	73
Let God Handle Your Light Weight!	79
Love Hell Right Out Of Them!	85
Giving That Pleases God	91
Prayer Is Not An Option–It's A Necessity!	95
Praying God's Way	101
Let It Go!!	113
The Spiritual Significance Of Fasting	119
Earthly Pleasures Or Heavenly Treasures?	125
Who Are You Going To Serve?	131
Don't Worry, And Let The Lord Handle It!	137
Check Yourself, Before You Wreck Yourself	143
The Preciousness Of The Word of God	149
The Keys To Receiving From God	155
The Golden Rule	159
Salvation Is A Decision	163
Watch Out For Wolves!	167
Part-Time Members In A Full-Time Church!	173
How's Your Foundation?	179
Bibliography	187

Principles of
KINGDOM LIVING
How to Live Right in a World Gone Wrong

CHAPTER 1

GOING THROUGH!

"And seeing the multitudes, he went up into a mountain: and when he was set, his disciples came unto him: And he opened up his mouth, and taught them saying, Blessed are the poor in spirit: for theirs is the Kingdom of Heaven. Blessed are they that mourn: for they shall be comforted. Blessed are the meek: for they shall inherit the earth."

Matthew 5:1-5

Do you know anything about "going through?" Many of us have been going through for some time now. It would appear that as soon as we get done with one thing, something else shows up! We can't seem to catch a break and have some time to rest and relax.

- Some of us are going through with our spouses

- Some of us are going through with our children
- Some of us are going through with our neighbors
- Some of us are going through with our jobs
- Some of us are going through with our co-workers
- Some of us are going through with our health
- Some of us are going through with our finances
- Some of us are going through with church folks, and believe it or not
- Some of us are going through with ourselves! We don't like the way we look; don't like the way things are going; we don't like how we're treated by others; we don't like the hand that life has dealt us up to this point. We find ourselves…Going Through!!!

I want to help somebody today and make all of us aware that life was never promised to be easy. I believe we need to go through a few things in order for us to understand and appreciate all that God has done and is doing for us. Again–

- We'll never understand what it's like to have a good day if we've never had a bad day
- We'll never understand what it's like to be healthy unless we've been sick
- We'll never understand what it's like to be happy unless we've been sad
- We'll never understand what it's like to have money unless we've been broke
- Can I get a witness?

One of the key truths we all must come to grips with is that this place, meaning earth, is not our home. We are merely "pilgrims passing through" and in doing so, we must learn and understand how to navigate our way along the journey.

Jesus knew that coming to this world He would be faced with many different obstacles and adversities, yet He came anyway. His mission was to die for

Going Through!

our sins and rise on the third day as was prophesied, but He also knew that some days would be better than others. Since He went through and we're still here, it would stand to reason that we're still Going Through!! But the question is…How will you deal with "Going Through?"

Our text is found in the Gospel of Matthew. Here in Chapter 5, Jesus is beginning what has been known throughout the ages as "The Sermon on the Mount." In the beginning of the chapter, Jesus is teaching what's called the Beatitudes and it's a series of conditions that people go through and what they can anticipate. I've learned and am learning that the difference between a good day and a bad is our own attitude. We can allow the situation to control us, or we can take control of the situation. I understand that we're humans and emotional beings, but we also have the ability and potential to not allow things and situations to get the best of us.

Concerning the Beatitudes, the first thing the Lord says about all of them is, "Blessed…" He's addressing the situations we go through and promises a positive outcome as we endure those challenges in life. Dr. Herbert Lockyer, in his book *All the Promises of the Bible* says, *"Already we have suggested that all the "Blesseds" of the Bible can be treated as promises, and here is one of them. Whatever future application this promise may have, the Christ can claim it now."*[1]

The word "Blessed" comes from the Greek word "makarios" and it means spiritual joy and satisfaction that lasts regardless of conditions; that carries one through pain, sorrow, loss, and grief.[2] When you're going through, you need something and someone to hold on to; something to get you through; someone to bring you through, and if you know that there's a blessing waiting for you, it makes the going through a whole lot easier to deal with.

Let's see who the Lord says are blessed. He starts out with:

Those Poor In Spirit (verse 3)

If we're not careful, this verse can be misunderstood very quickly. Some may take the word "poor" and the phrase "Kingdom of Heaven" to mean that the only way to enter into the Kingdom of Heaven is to be poor. It's

[1] Herbert Lockyer, All The Promises of the Bible
[2] Preacher's Outline and Sermon Bible, Matthew 1, page 54

important that we look at the entire verse to see what it actually says. Jesus is making reference to the "poor in spirit" which are those who are in spiritual poverty. This is the person who recognizes that he or she is completely and totally dependent on God for all their needs, wants, and desires. They realize that it's not about "my three favorite people…me, myself, and I" rather what and who God desires me to be. They don't operate in pride and living a puffed-up life, but know that their true blessings come from God. The Bible says in Proverbs 16:18, *"Pride goeth before destruction, and an haughty spirit before a fall."* Jesus promises that if we are poor in spirit, the Kingdom of Heaven is promised to us. We're told in Romans 8:15-17, *"For ye have not received the spirit of bondage again to fear; but ye have received the Spirit of adoption, whereby we cry, Abba, Father. The Spirit itself beareth witness with our spirit, that we are the children of God: and if children, then heirs; heirs of God, and joint-heirs with Christ; if so be that we suffer with him, that we may be also glorified together."* It's not a matter of being poor financially, but about being dependent on God for all things, thereby positioning ourselves to receive the Kingdom of Heaven.

Those Who Mourn (verse 4)

To mourn is to have a broken heart. I believe all of us would agree that when a loved one transitions from this life to eternal life, it has an effect on our hearts. *The Preacher's Outline and Sermon Bible* gives us at least three people who mourn:

- *"Those who are desperately sorry for his sins and unworthiness before God*
- *Those who really feels the desperate plight and terrible suffering of others and,*
- *Those who experiences personal tragedy and intense trauma"* [3]

If it hasn't happened yet, keep living and the opportunity to mourn will come knocking on the door of your heart! Jesus says that those who mourn will be comforted. Again, it is a condition with promise and He always keeps His promises. He knows what it's like to mourn or be in sorrow because the Bible says that would apply to Him. We find in Isaiah 53:3, *"He is despised and rejected of men; a man of sorrows, and acquainted with*

[3] Ibid, page 57

grief: and we hid as it were our faces from him; he was despised, and we esteemed him not." But even though that happened to Him, He still makes the promise of comforting His people. When you are mourning, you need something to hold on to and look forward to and the Bible promises us in Psalm 16:11, *"Thou will show me the path of life; in thy presence is fullness of joy; at thy right hand there are pleasures for evermore."* When you are going through your mourning season, you may need something the world can't give you; but Jesus promises to comfort you like nobody can!!

<u>Those Who Are Meek (verse 5)</u>

Let me take a minute to clarify something, meekness is not weakness as some people think it is. They have the tendency of thinking that because a person is meek–you know–kind, gentle, easy going, never gets upset about things, that they can be taken advantage of, and will try to do it when they feel the opportunity presents itself. Actually, to be meek is to be strong. It means to have a *"strong, but tender, and humble life."*[4] A meek person is a disciplined person with the ability to be strong and able to take and conquer, yet understands they are God-controlled and operates from God's perspective. The Apostle Paul talks about that control when he said in 1 Corinthians 9:27, *"But I keep under my body, and bring it into subjection: lest by any means, when I have preached to others, I myself should be a castaway."* He's telling us it does him no good if he can tell people about the Lord, yet does nothing personally to follow the Lord. Jesus tells us that the meek shall inherit the earth. What exactly does that mean? I'm glad you asked that question…it means two things:

- The meek will enjoy and experience the good things of the earth now.[5] The Bible says in Philippians 1:6, *"Being confident of this very thing, that he which hath begun a good work in you will perform it unto the day of Jesus Christ."* You see, the meek have nothing to prove to anybody but the Lord and they are very comfortable in their own skins. Are you comfortable with who you are? If we are spending all of our time pleasing others, we will make ourselves miserable before we know it!

- The meek understands that the earth will be theirs eternally![6] This pertains to the promises of the new heaven and the new earth

[4]Ibid, page 57 - [5]Ibid, page 59 - [6]Ibid, page 60

that God has promised! The Apostle John tells us in Revelation 21:1, *"And I saw a new heaven and a new earth: for the first heaven and the first earth were passed away."*

So it's not a matter of what you're going through, it's really a matter of the promise of the Lord that you will make it through. He never promised us it would be easy, but He has told us He can make it easier to endure. He promised us in Matthew 11:28-30, *"Come unto me, all ye that labour and are heavy laden, and I will give you rest. Take my yoke upon you, and learn of me; for I am meek and lowly in heart: and ye shall find rest unto your souls. For my yoke is easy, and my burden is light."*

Principles of
KINGDOM LIVING
How to Live Right in a World Gone Wrong

CHAPTER 2

THRIVING

"Blessed are they which do hunger and thirst after righteousness: for they shall be filled. Blessed are the merciful: for they shall obtain mercy.

Blessed are the pure in heart: for they shall see God."

Matthew 5:6-9

In the previous chapter, I shared the fact that while here on planet earth, we will, at some point in time, find ourselves going through some things. Life has a way of throwing the proverbial monkey wrench at us and sometimes, messes us up in more ways than one. The difference between someone coming out on the other side of going through, is how that person responds to life's monkey wrenches. One of the things we can do is wallow in our problems or obstacles, take on a defeated mentality, and just give up; or we can get up, shake it off, and make the most of what's coming at us. To do this, we must have the right attitude, or even a change of attitude.

- The defeated person has made up their mind that they are already defeated
- The defeated person has made up their mind that they will never get any better
- The defeated person has made up their mind that they will never get any help
- The defeated person has made up their mind that there's no hope for them

On the other hand…

- The thriving person has made up their mind that defeat is not an option
- The thriving person has made up their mind that whatever comes their way will be conquered
- The thriving person has made up their mind to go after what is rightfully theirs
- The thriving person has made up their mind that victory is imminent!

Let me ask a few questions:

- If/when you lose your job, do you stop living?
- If/when you lose a loved one, do you stop living?
- If/when you lose something near and dear to you do you stop living?

No! You understand that it's all part of the life cycle we're in and you keep living!!! There are some who feel that life is over when these things happen, yet the person who thrives sees things from an entirely different perspective!

I would submit to you that the difference is a matter of attitude! It's an attitude that helps us to understand that God knows what's best for me and mine and I'm willing to let Him direct my path. We take on the attitude that according to Psalm 119:105 which says, *"Thy word is a lamp unto my feet, and a light unto my path."* God knows what's best and that gives us a thriving attitude!!

In verses 3-5 of Matthew 5, Jesus is dealing with someone who I characterized as "going through" because of all the things being added to them. In each one, Jesus reminds them that in their "going through," there was a promise of something better, if they just stuck it out! In the first three, something was coming at the individual, or they were in a particular state of mind or being. In the next three verses, Jesus begins dealing with the individual who understands that the past is actually preparing them for their future and they need to do something to thrive!

<u>*Those Who Hunger and Thirst (verse 6)*</u>

Let me ask a question here–when you are at home (or wherever), when you get hungry, what do you do? When you get thirsty what do you do? Most people when they get hungry at home, get up, go into the kitchen, and find something to eat! Most people, when they are thirsty at home, get up, go into the kitchen, and find something to drink! Most people when they get hungry at work, if they don't bring lunch with them, they get up, go somewhere, and get something to eat. My point being, they are not sitting around waiting for food to come to them in order to deal with their hunger, but they get up and do something. A person who thrives will not sit on the sidelines and wait for things to happen for them, but will get up, get moving, and make something happen for themselves. The text refers to the one who has a hunger and thirst after righteousness, and that includes all righteousness! This is the person who wants to do what's right even though wrong keeps coming at them. They've made it up in their mind that they are going to be righteous in their dealings and do things God's way, not their own way. In this case, we thrive to be more like Jesus!!

The Preacher's Outline and Sermon Bible says, "In the Bible, righteousness means two simple but profound things; it has a double meaning. It means <u>to be</u> right and <u>to do</u> right. It may be said another way: <u>to be</u> good and to do good."[7] Here's what real—we can't be righteous on our own because the Bible teaches us in Isaiah 64:6, *"But we are all as an unclean thing, and all our righteousnesses are as filthy rags; and we all do fade as a leaf; and our iniquities, like the wind, have taken us away."* King David said in Psalm 51:5, *"Behold, I was shapen in iniquity; and in sin did my mother conceive me."* Because sin has been passed down since Adam, we've got to change our attitude and make it up in our minds that we will hunger and thirst after righteousness, thereby hungering and thirsting to be more like Jesus! The promise from the Lord is that if we have that hunger and thirst, we shall be filled!!! What will we be filled with? The Bible tells us in:

- Romans 15:14, we will be filled with goodness and all knowledge
- Ephesians 3:19, we will be filled with the fullness of God
- Ephesians 5:18, we will be filled with the Spirit
- Philippians 1:11, we will be filled with the fruits of righteousness
- Colossians 1:9, we will be filled with the knowledge of His [God's] will
- Acts 13:52, we will be filled with joy and with the Holy Spirit

Then and only then can we really....THRIVE!!!

Those Who Are Merciful (verse 7)

When somebody does something wrong to you, from a natural perspective, it's difficult to forgive them, or have mercy on them. You're hurting; you're devastated; you're not sure what has happened; so it's difficult to be merciful at that moment. To be merciful is to have a compassionate heart and a forgiving spirit. The person who is merciful makes a deliberate effort to understand the person who needs forgiveness. If we are going to Thrive, we've got to change our attitude and begin to function and operate like Jesus because...

- There will come a time when people will talk about you
- There will come a time when people spread rumors on you

---

[7] Ibid, Deeper Study #5, page 61

- There will come a time when people will judge you wrongly
- There will come a time when people will drag your name through the mud
- There will come a time when people will lie on you
- There will come a time when people will call you everything but a child of God

But the real question is what will do you when that happens?

Jesus says here that the merciful will receive mercy. By definition, mercy comes from a Greek word which means *"feelings of pity, compassion, affection, and kindness."* When we show mercy to others it will in turn come back to us. It's the principle of sowing and reaping found in Galatians 6:7 which says, *"Be not deceived, God is not mocked; for whatsoever a man soweth, that shall he also reap."*[8] There are benefits of showing mercy to others. The Bible tells us that:

- You will receive the mercy of God
- You will be paid back given by God Himself
- You will be blessed
- You will inherit the Kingdom of God

When we start following the Word of God and living in a manner that's pleasing to God, it is then that we start Thriving!

Those Who Are Pure in Heart (verse 8)

Another way for us to thrive is to be pure in heart. *The Preacher's Outline and Sermon Bible* says that this means *"to have a clean heart; to be unsoiled, unmixed, unpolluted; to be cleansed, purged, forgiven."* [8]The only way we can be pure in heart is to know Christ as savior and allow Him to live through us. It requires us to make it up in our minds to live holy before God, forgetting those things behind; those things that have hurt us; those who have messed over us, those who have turned their backs on us! We can't succumb to doing things the world's way, but realize there's a better

---

[8]Ibid, page 62

way with God. 1 Peter 1:22 says, *"Seeing ye have purified your souls in obeying the truth through the Spirit unto unfeigned love of the brethren, see that ye love one another with a pure heart fervently."*...If we do it God's way, we can anticipate the blessings from God. The Bible says in Psalms 24:4-5, *"He that hath clean hands, and a pure heart; who hath not lifted up his soul unto vanity, nor sworn deceitfully. He shall receive the blessing from the Lord, and righteousness from the God of his salvation."* But the text tells us that the pure in heart shall see God. What a promise that is? We can look forward to seeing God face to face, beholding His glory and His glory and His glory. We're told in Psalm 17:15, *"As for me, I will behold thy face in righteousness: I shall be satisfied, when I wake, with thy likeness."* Can you imagine what it's going to be like, waking up on the other side of eternity and seeing God face to face? It will happen for those who are pure in heart!

Thriving requires us to get up, shake it off, and get to stepping! You can't thrive if you're walking around with a defeated attitude; you can't thrive if you're taking out revenge on people who have offended or hurt you; you can't thrive if your heart is not right!

Even though Jesus was *"wounded for our transgressions and bruised for our iniquities,"* He had His mind set on thriving!

You want to talk about thriving? Let's talk about what He endured:

- He was betrayed by a friend
- He was sold for 30 pieces of silver
- He was forsaken by His disciples
- He was accused by false witnesses
- He was mocked and beaten
- He was pierced in His hands and feet
- He was crucified between two thieves
- He was the object of ridicule
- He was deserted or forsaken by God

Thriving

- He died on Calvary's cross
- He didn't just stay in the grave, but got up early on Sunday morning with all power in His hands

If you're going to thrive, you've got to get up! Maybe you might need to get up and praise God! Maybe you might need to get up and worship God! Maybe you need to get up and tell Him "thank you!" Maybe you might need to get up and say "hallelujah!"

Principles of Kingdom Living

Principles of
KINGDOM LIVING
How to Live Right in a World Gone Wrong

CHAPTER
3

TRIUMPHING

"Blessed are the peacemakers: for they shall be called the children of God."

Blessed are they which are persecuted for righteousness' sake: for theirs is the Kingdom of Heaven. Blessed are ye, when men shall revile you, and persecute you, and shall say all manner of evil against you falsely, for my sake. Rejoice, and be exceeding glad: for great is your reward in heaven: for so persecuted they the prophets which were before you."

Matthew 5:9-12

I think I need to start off this chapter by saying that it never has been nor will it ever be God's intention that we live in defeat, or less than to our full potential. For some reason, we have gotten to the point of accepting certain situations in life as being influenced by the devil and we accept the outcome without understanding that even though they may have been influenced by the devil, God allowed them to take place so we could in fact begin to operate to our full potential in Him! Even when those situations come our way, when we confront and handle them God's way, we're guaranteed success because there's no failure in God. That means we can live a life in triumph, and never in defeat!

By definition, the word triumph means, *"to be victorious or successful; to rejoice; exult."*[9] Being in Christ affords us the opportunity to see the mighty power of the Lord right before our very eyes, as we see our troubles and trials turn into triumphs.

As we continue in Matthew 5, we find that the Lord has made promises to people who have and will experience certain things. He dealt with the poor in spirit, those who mourn, those who are meek, they that hunger and thirst after righteousness, those who are merciful, and the pure in heart. For each instance, the Lord promises them something that the world can't give them, but rewards that come directly from heaven! I can handle a promise like that!! But again, in order for us to obtain those heavenly blessings, we will have to be exposed to some of the challenges of life. And let us remember that the challenge is not there to destroy us, but to make us better for God and for the kingdom's sake. Let's look at the text.

Jesus said Blessed are…

<u>Those Who are Peacemakers (verse 9)</u>

I have learned and am learning that it takes two people to fight, argue, and have disputes with one another. Some people will pick a fight just for the sake of picking a fight, while others will engage in that behavior to prove they are right or prove their point. None of us are perfect and we can't expect that we will be right all the time. I would submit that there are times when you are right, but if you would be honest with yourself, you will also find that you are wrong sometimes too! And of course that works both ways! Sometimes it takes a bigger person to admit to being wrong, being sorry, and moving on beyond the situation. This person can be considered

[9] American Heritage Dictionary, Third Edition

a peacemaker. One definition of a peacemaker is *"one who makes peace, especially by settling disputes."*[10] Can I be real here? There are times when we deal with some people and all we want to do is send them to meet their maker, "NCIS slap" them in the back of their heads, or try to destroy them by telling other people all the dirt you have on them. Obviously, this is not making or establishing peace, but trying to take matters into our own hands. And if I can help somebody, the time to react or respond to somebody is not always immediately because a response in anger is not responding in a godly manner. The Bible teaches us in Romans 14:19, *"Let us therefore follow after the things which make for peace, and things wherewith one may edify another."* Our motive should be handle things the way we believe God would want things done. He's told us in Philippians 2:3, *"Let nothing be done through strife or vainglory; but in lowliness of mind let each esteem others better than ourselves."* Jesus says here, *"Blessed are the peacemakers,"* not "Blessed are the fight starters!" The promise here for the peacemakers is that they shall be called the "children of God." Children of God are part of the family of God and that means entitlements and benefits. When you are a child of God, you can:

- Call on Him when you can't call on anybody else
- Expect Him to hear and have the power to answer your prayer
- Anticipate His presence around you all the time
- See Him moving obstacles and opposition right out of your way
- Feel Him strengthen you when you begin to feel weak
- Know that He loves and will be there for you

In the natural, if you get locked up, your earthly father can bail you out! With God, when life tries to put you on lock-down, God can make you so free, you'll be free indeed!!! If you want these benefits, you must be a peacemaker.

<u>Those Who are Persecuted and Reviled (verses 10-11)</u>

Let me ask a question here, do you know anything about being persecuted? Persecution takes place anywhere and practically everywhere we go.

---

[10] American Heritage Dictionary, Third Edition

Principles of Kingdom Living

Sometimes we're persecuted for where we live; sometimes we are persecuted because of the jobs we have; sometimes we're persecuted because of the friends we have; and there are so many other reasons why people would intentionally come after us or attack us. Because we're human, we should anticipate that we will have "haters" out there, but Jesus is referring to those who are persecuted for righteousness sake. He's talking about those who take a stand for the gospel and not bow down to peer pressure or political correctness.

In these days and times we're living in, we can all see and experience what it's like to be persecuted for righteousness sake. The Bible teaches us in 2 Timothy 3:12, *"Yea, and all that will live godly shall suffer persecution."* As I thought about what's taken place in recent history, I came across something on Facebook that ties in to this. The statement goes (and I'm paraphrasing), "Tim Tebow professes to be a Christian and he's told to keep that to himself; yet Jason Collins admits to being gay and the current President of the United States, a former president of the United States, and the NBA Commissioner all applauded him for admitting to his alternate lifestyle." Do you think Tim Tebow has been persecuted for righteousness sake? What about the people on their jobs who want to talk about Jesus during breaks or share something special that happened during worship the day before and the job says you can't talk about Christ there? Yet, people can tell all the dirty jokes they can and talk about their "weekend encounters" without persecution whatsoever! Jesus wants us to know that we're in good company for being persecuted for righteousness sake because He was persecuted as well! He told us in John 15:18, *"If the world hate you, ye know that it hated me before it hated you."*

The person who is persecuted for righteousness sake, Jesus says, *"theirs is the Kingdom of God."* What can be found in the Kingdom of God? I'm glad you asked that question! The Bible teaches us that in the Kingdom of God, there is:

No Corruption

No Curse

No Killing or Death

Triumphing

No More Sorrow

No Thieves or Stealing

No Defilement or Wickedness

No More Pain and Suffering

You'll inherit a mansion; and be with Jesus throughout all eternity!!! But keep in mind, you will endure some persecution in order to get to the Kingdom of Heaven.

When you are a peacemaker it empowers you to be triumphant! When you are persecuted for righteousness sake it empowers you to be triumphant! We do know that we have to go through something in order to achieve the reward. Jesus tells us in verse 12 to, *"Rejoice and be exceedingly glad!"* And Guess what:

- When you have Jesus on your side you have a reason to rejoice
- When you know that Jesus has your back, you have a reason to rejoice
- When you know that what Jesus has promised will indeed come to pass you have a reason to rejoice

We can rejoice because the Bible teaches us in:

Psalm 5:11, *"But let all those that put their trust in thee rejoice;"*

Psalm 9:2, *"I will be glad and rejoice in thee: I will sing praise to thy name, O thou most High."*

Psalm 13:5, *"But I have trusted in thy mercy, my heart shall rejoice in thy salvation."*

Psalm 32:11, *"Be glad in the Lord, and rejoice, ye righteous: and shout for joy, all ye that are upright in heart."*

Jesus makes the difference in all of "your going through", enabling you to thrive, and making you triumphant!! He said in John 16:33, *"…In the world ye shall have tribulation: but be of good cheer: I have overcome the world."*

What has the Lord overcome?

- He's overcome being tempted by the devil
- He's overcome being betrayed by a friend
- He's overcome being falsely accused
- He's overcome being beaten till He was unrecognizable
- He's overcome being crucified on Calvary's cross
- He's overcome being buried in a borrowed tomb
- He's overcome death by rising early on Sunday morning
- He's coming back again with all power in His hands!!!
- Because He's triumphant, that makes us triumphant!!!

Principles of
KINGDOM LIVING
How to Live Right in a World Gone Wrong

CHAPTER

4

BEING A TRUE DISCIPLE

"Ye are the salt of the earth: but if the salt have lost his savour, wherewith shall it be salted? It is thenceforth good for nothing, but to be cast out, and to be trodden under foot of men."

Matthew 5:13

Anybody who loves to cook, or more importantly, loves to eat, knows what happens to food if you don't put enough seasoning on it. Once the plate is in front of you, you take that first bite of the food and immediately determine if it needs anything to help with the taste. If it is determined that there's something missing, you usually don't go looking for ground sage, or ground ginger, paprika, ground rosemary, ground thyme, or even creole seasoning – you usually go looking for salt and/or pepper! Some people like to add garlic salt or even lemon pepper to their food but because of the mixture, it doesn't always give the desired effect that true salt and pepper can deliver.

I said all that to say this, God doesn't need us adding outside things or the world's influence to ourselves because He wants us to be True Disciples for *His Kingdom*. Many people try to add things to make them appear to be more individualized but you can never be more of an individual than to be what and who God made you to be. Your life carries a certain level of distinctiveness with it and you are the only one who can truly be you!! God made you that way and wants to use you for *His Kingdom* purposes. He has made you and me to be "seasoning" in the earth to give it that distinctiveness He's looking for! Once we have accepted His Son, Jesus Christ, as Lord and Savior, all He wants is for us to be True Disciples!!!

So what is a true disciple? According to dictionary.com, the word true means to be *real, genuine, and authentic;"*[11] and the word disciple means *"a person who is a pupil or an adherent of the doctrines of another; a follower."*[12] So a true disciple therefore is one who is a real, genuine, and authentic pupil or adherent of the doctrines of another – in this case, Jesus Christ. It means we can't be fake, wishy-washy, some-timey, or part-time, but we must be real about what we learn from the Lord and put it to life on a daily basis!!!

As we continue through Matthew 5, we've come to that part of the sermon where Jesus is comparing the disciple to salt and how the two make a difference. Just as salt has no equal as it pertains to the various types of seasonings, so the true disciple has no equal as well. Salt is set aside or set apart for a particular use and purpose and that's what a true disciple is to God. When He saves us, one of the things we experience is called Sanctification, which is a separation unto God for a particular use and purpose. Once we've been sanctified, we don't go where we used to go, do what we used to do, say what we used to say, act like we used to act, instead, we begin to influence those around us because God has changed us for His purposes. We've become salt for God's glory! So if we want to be a true disciple we must know a few things about salt.

<u>Salt's Character</u>[13] When I was in the military, there were some people that we called "salty." These were people who had been around for a while, but more importantly, whatever they said or did was a reflection of the military

[11]Dictionary.com - [12]Ibid
[13]Preacher's Outline and Sermon Bible, Matthew 1, Outline Topics Only

in them. When they answered a question, it had a military influence; when they were out of uniform, they wore something that made reference to the Marine Corps; even after hours, they spoke to you in military time – if you were going to meet them somewhere, they would set the time at 1900 instead of 7 p.m. It set them apart from just the ordinary person in uniform. Here's a few things about salt we want to look at:

> **Salt is Distinctive** There is no other ingredient like it in the world and that can be said of true disciples. As true disciples, we are called and designed to be the salt of the earth and God wants us to be *"unspotted from the world."* In 2 Corinthians 6:17-18 we find, *"Wherefore come out from among them, and be ye separate, saith the Lord, and touch not the unclean thing; and I will receive you, and will be a Father unto you, and ye shall be my sons and daughters, saith the Lord Almighty."*

> **Salt Preserves** To preserve means to keep from going bad or being destroyed. Although I've never had to do it, I've heard of stories when people who lived in the country used to kill their food and coat the meat in salt as a way to preserve it. They didn't have freezers like we do today, but they did have salt to keep their meat fresh. God has called us to be a preservative to the world to keep it fresh and save it from corruption. The Bible teaches us in 1 Peter 1:22-25, *"22 Seeing ye have purified your souls in obeying the truth through the Spirit unto unfeigned love of the brethren, see that ye love one another with a pure heart fervently: 23 Being born again, not of corruptive seed, but of incorruptible, by the Word of God, which liveth and abideth for ever. 24 For all flesh is as grass, and all the glory of man as the flower of grass. The grass withereth, and the flower thereof falleth away: 25 But the word of the Lord endureth forever. And this is the word which by the gospel is preached unto you."* It's the word that helps us to preserve!!

> **Salt Penetrates** When salt touches the food we eat, it penetrates it so that the flavor is found throughout. That's how God wants us to be in the world, with the ability to penetrate and influence people to see things God's way. Once this happens, a new quality, substance, and life takes place. We're told in Ephesians 4:24, *"And that ye put*

Principles of Kingdom Living

on the new man, which after God is created in righteousness and true holiness."

> **<u>Salt Flavors</u>** Most places you go to eat at cook their food without seasoning, and therefore the food is bland. I can't speak for anyone else, but I can't stand eating bland food! On the other hand, I enjoy eating a good steak that requires no steak sauce at all – why? Because it has the right amount of flavor already in it! Salt is that ingredient which adds flavor like no other and that's how the Lord wants to use us with our fellow man. 1 John 1:3 says, *"That which we have seen and heard declare we unto you, that ye also may have fellowship with us: and truly our fellowship is with the Father and with His Son Jesus Christ."*

> **<u>Salt Spreads</u>** When you shake salt onto food it goes all over it. It doesn't just stop in one spot but makes its way everywhere. As the salt of the earth, we should always be mindful of our commission to evangelize the world. 1 Peter 3:15 says, *"But sanctify the Lord God in your hearts: and be ready to always give an answer to every man that asketh you a reason of the hope that is in you with meekness and fear."*

> **<u>Salt is Irrepressible</u>** One thing that can be said about salt is that once you put it out there you can't take it back. It goes forth with purpose and does what it set out to do. So is the Word of God as found in Isaiah 55:11 which says, *"So shall my word be that goeth forth out of my mouth: it shall not return unto me void, but it shall accomplish that which I please, and it shall prosper in the thing whereto I sent it."* As the salt of the earth, God wants to use us to get His Word out!!

<u>**Salt's Ministry**</u> If you take a close look at our selected text, you will find that the Lord gave a specific location for salt to be used – the earth! Since this is where we live the earth is the place in which we can have the most influence. After the Resurrection of Jesus Christ, He told His Disciples to meet Him in Jerusalem so that He could empower them for their work. Once they were all assembled in Jerusalem, He told them in Acts 1:8, *"But ye shall receive power, after that the Holy Ghost is come upon you: and*

Being A True Disciple

ye shall be witnesses unto me both in Jerusalem, and in all Judea, and in Samaria, and unto the uttermost part of the earth." Here the Lord details for them where their ministry was supposed to be. Since we don't have those places around us, we do have the place in which we live to spread our "salt" in the earth.

It has been reported recently that there are approximately 33 million unchurched people in the state of California alone. This means those people do not attend church at all, or may only attend for special holidays, weddings, or funerals. They have no religious or denominational affiliation and are destined for eternal damnation if they do not make a decision to accept and receive Christ as Lord and Savior before leaving earth. That's why the Bible teaches us in Matthew 9:37-38, *"Then saith he unto his disciples, The hearvest truly is plenteous, but the labourers are few; 38 Pray ye therefore the Lord of the harvest that he will send forth labourers into his harvest."* I can't speak for anybody else, but I'm so glad somebody spread some salt around me so I can know Jesus Christ for myself!!! – Amen!!!

<u>Salt's Mission.</u> *The Preacher's Outline and Sermon Bible* says, *"the disciples' mission is to salt the earth. Note a critical point: believers are the salt of the earth, not of heaven. They can do nothing to salt heaven. They cannot penetrate, flavor, or preserve heaven. Any relationship whatsoever they have with heaven is a gift from heaven. However, believers are the salt of the earth; they can penetrate, flavor, and preserve the earth."*[14] For this to be true, the Believer cannot do these things unless they have "salt" in them already!!

> - You can't tell somebody about a Savior that you don't know
> - You can't tell somebody about a Healer who has never healed you
> - You can't tell somebody about a Redeemer unless you've been redeemed already
> - You can't tell somebody about Eternal Life unless you already have it

As salt, we have the mission to go and tell somebody about the One who has made us the "salt of the earth" and His name is Jesus. Not only did He give us a mission, but He commissioned us to be salt. He commissioned us

---

[14]Preacher's Outline and Sermon Bible, Matthew 1, page 67

Principles of Kingdom Living

in Matthew 28:19-20 when He said, *"Go ye therefore and teach all nations, baptizing them in the name of the Father, and of the Son, and of the Holy Ghost: 20 Teaching them to observe all things whatsoever I have commanded you: and lo, I am with you alway, even unto the end of the world."*

One thing we must be mindful of and that is our usefulness! Although salt cannot lose its saltiness or flavor, it can become useless when mixed with the wrong things. When Jesus was giving this statement, salt was gathered in certain places to be used at the appropriate time. There were times when the salt was mixed in with the dirt and was no longer useful, and actually became destructive to the ground it was found in. It is critical for us to understand that we don't need to be mixed in with the world, nor take on the plans and vices of the world in order to be used by God! This statement also has a reference to backsliders, or those who have known the Lord, but have turned their backs on Him. Of this person, God says in Hebrews 10:38, *"Now the just shall live by faith: but if any man draw back, my soul shall have no pleasure in him."*

So if you want to be a true disciple, you've got to be salty!

- You've got to live a life reflective of the One who gave you Eternal Life
- You've got to be distinctive
- You've got to be a preserver
- You've got to be a penetrator and allow the Word of God penetrate the heart and soul of mankind
- You've got to add flavor
- You've got to spread yourself out
- You've got to be irrepressible

If you want to be a true disciple:

- You've got to tell a dying world about a Risen Savior
- You've got to tell the world about the King of kings, and Lord of Lords

Being A True Disciple

- You've got to tell the world about the Great I AM
- You've got to tell the world about the Door of the Sheep
- You've got to tell the world about the Good Shepherd
- You've got to tell the world about the Lily of the Valley, and the Bright and Morning Star
- You've got to tell the world about the One who hung, bled, and died on Calvary's Cross between two thieves
- You've got to tell the world about the One who was put in a borrowed tomb
- You've got to tell the world about the One who Rose from the dead early one Sunday morning with all Power in His hands
- You've got to tell the world about Jesus!
- You've got to tell the world about Jesus!

Then and only then, will you be a true disciple!!!

Principles of Kingdom Living

Principles of
KINGDOM LIVING
How to Live Right in a World Gone Wrong

CHAPTER
5

TURN ON THE LIGHT!

"Ye are the light of the world. A city that is set on an hill cannot be hid. Neither do men light a candle, and put it under a bushel, but on a candlestick; and it giveth light unto all that are in the house. Let your light so shine before men, that they may see your good works, and glorify your Father which is in heaven."

Matthew 5:14-16

I grew up in a part of New Orleans whereby we frequently had uninvited guests at the house. These guests had the tendency to come around when we were not around, or after we went to sleep. You really didn't know they were there until you walked into the kitchen and turned the light on. It was then that they realized they were uninvited, turned around, and started running! These uninvited guests I'm referring to are known scientifically as *"Periplaneta Americana,"* but we know them as the common household cockroach!

You may be asking yourself, "why did he bring up such a pest as the cockroach?" I'm glad you asked that question. I brought up the cockroach because it symbolizes how sin operates in our lives.

- When we least expect it–it shows up
- When we think it's not there–it's there
- When we deal with it–it runs and flees

But we must understand that sin will flee from us when we have the right deterrent for it and that is the Light of God.

Here in our text, Jesus is continuing His Sermon on the Mount. He's already told the masses that they are Blessed when they endure certain challenges and obstacles in life. It's encouraging to know that:

- When you mourn–you will be comforted
- When you are poor in spirit–the Kingdom of Heaven is yours
- When you are meek–you shall inherit the earth
- When you hunger and thirst after Righteousness, you shall be filled

Now, the Lord addresses the believer and gives a command to believers as well. He tells the believer to *"Let your light so shine before men"* which is a clear indication that He expects them to do something with it. It's kind of like the expectation of a parent who sends their child off to school; and because they are attending on a daily basis, the expectation is that they will learn something while there. Jesus prefaced that statement by saying, *"Ye are the light of the world"* which would also tell us that there must be a purpose for the Light. Let's take a look at light and see what we can glean from it.

If we are going to "Turn on the Light," we must understand a few things first.

Turn On The Light!

Light Requires An Energy Source

A light bulb by itself is of no real use and value except to take up space, but when you put it in a receptacle and plug it in, the light can be used properly. As the Light of the world, we must understand that our effectiveness is of little use and value if we are not plugged into the *right* energy source. In 1 John 1:5, the Bible teaches us, *"This then is the message which we have heard of him, and declare unto you, that God is light, and in him is no darkness at all."* Not only is God Light, but so is Jesus Christ. He reminds us in John 8:12, *"I am the light of the world: he that followeth me shall not walk in darkness, but shall have the light of life."* If we are going to **Turn on the Light**, we've got to make sure we have the *right* energy source. I can't speak for you, but Jesus is my energy source and I'm glad He doesn't turn off! If you don't pay your electric bill, they will turn off your energy source or electricity until you get back in a good status with them, but when you have been connected with Christ, that energy source is *always available* because the Bible teaches us in Hebrews 13:8, *"Jesus Christ the same yesterday, and to day, and for ever."* I was watching the news one day and saw a story about a lady whose car was swallowed up by a sink hole. She said the entire time her car was going into the hole, she didn't call on her family or her friends, but kept calling on the name of Jesus, Jesus, Jesus! She walked away unharmed, yet her car needed lots of work. You see, when you are connected to the *right* energy source, the power shows up at the *right* time all the time! It's time to **Turn On The Light!!!**

Light Has Only One Purpose

When you enter into a dark room one of the first things you do is look for the light switch, or if you know where it is, you turn on the light. When the light comes on, it dispels the darkness, and much like roaches, makes the darkness scatter. The purpose of light is to dispel darkness and keep it away from you. That's why it's so important for us to **Turn on the Light** that Christ has given to us. When Jesus came to planet earth, His mission, aside from dying for your sins and mine and rising early on Sunday morning was to Bring Light into the world. John 1:4-5 says, *"In him was life; and the life was the light of men. And the light shineth in darkness; and the darkness comprehended it not."* It's interesting that when the Lord came on the scene, people still wanted to do their own thing! They wanted to hold on to their selfish ways; they wanted to hold on to their traditions, even to the point whereby they were so closed minded that they didn't even want to consider what Jesus was saying! Well, there's nothing new under the sun–we've had the Light of Christ in the world for over two thousand years now and people *still* want to do their own thing. This is evident today with the recent turn of events with regard to same-sex marriage, the insistence of Islam trying to force their religion on the world, and how it appears that there's no real stability in the world anymore. Light comes to expose the darkness and then the darkness responds by doing its own thing. We can call it rebellion and there's plenty of that in our society right now! Proverbs 4:19 says, *"The way of the wicked is as darkness: they know not at what they stumble."* When light comes on it has a way of helping the wicked and us to see better and show us the way. We're told in Psalm 119:105, *"Thy word is a lamp unto my feet, and a light unto my path."* When we Turn On the Light, we can see the true purpose of the light!

Light Cannot Be Hidden

Sometimes things are hidden as a means of protecting them or preserving them from bad or evil things or people. That is not the case as it pertains to light, especially the Light that Christ gives us. If you take a lit light bulb and cover it up, you can still see some of the light coming through whatever you used to cover it with. When you have the Light of Christ working *within* you it cannot be covered up, nor can it be hidden. I believe we must be careful regarding that because we sometimes hide the Light that's in us. I'll give you an example, you attend worship Sunday after Sunday, yet you go to work Monday thru Friday and nobody knows that you have accepted Christ as Lord and Savior. When the topic finally comes up, people are shocked and surprised by this revelation and never knew about your relationship with Christ. I say all the time that I'm glad somebody shared Christ with me and I now have eternal life through Him. They didn't hide their light, but rather shared it with me. I'll also share this, some years ago, I came across a vehicle that had various Masonic symbols on it. The owner of the vehicle saw me looking at it and I enquired about the symbols, to which he responded, that's my light!" I found it interesting that people don't have a problem sharing false light, but it becomes a problem sometimes

Turn On The Light!

when it comes to sharing the Truth!! The text here says, *"Neither do men light a candle, and put it under a bushel, but on a candlestick; and it giveth light unto all that are in the house."* The idea here is that when we Turn on the Light, we are not to hide it but rather lift it up high so that others can see the Light that's coming from us. The Apostle Paul reminds us in 2 Corinthians 4:6, *"For God, who commanded the light to shine out of darkness, hath shined in our hearts, to give the light of the knowledge of the glory of God in the face of Jesus Christ."* What am I trying to say:

- If the Lord has Saved your soul–you need to tell somebody about it
- If the Lord has Made you whole–you need to tell somebody about it
- If the Lord has Healed your body–you need to tell somebody about it
- If the Lord has Delivered you–you need to tell somebody about it
- If the Lord has Protected you–you need to tell somebody about it
- If the Lord has been better to you than you can be to yourself–you need to tell somebody about it
- If the Lord has been there for you like nobody else–you need to tell somebody about it
- If the Lord is Coming back for you one day–you need to tell somebody about it

If we are going to be true to what the Lord requires of us, we will have to make it up in our minds that we are going to do it, regardless of ridicule, regardless of how people think of us and regardless of the outcome. As the people of God, we are quick to recite what we see in Psalm 46:1-3 which reads,

> *"God is our refuge and strength, a very present help in trouble. Therefore will not we fear, though the earth be removed, and though the mountains be carried into the midst of the sea; Though the waters thereof roar and be troubled, though the mountains shake with the swelling thereof."*

But, are we really willing to do what's required of us from the Lord? The devil wants you to be afraid and he works best when you are at that point in your life. God's Word has told us in 2 Timothy 1:7, *"For God hath not given us a spirit of fear; but of power, and of love, and of a sound mind."* Therefore, we should not be afraid to share our faith, share our hope, and definitely share our Christ with others. Jesus went before the devil; He went before Caiaphas the high priest, and Pontius Pilate for your sins and mine! He wasn't afraid of the outcome because He is the Overcomer, and so are we *if* we are in Him and let our lights shine! Again, today, it's time to Turn On The Light!!!

We're Commanded to Let It Shine

When Jesus said, *"Let your light shine...,"* it was not a suggestion or recommendation. Generally speaking, sometimes people think that the only commands we've been given in Scripture are found in Exodus 20 where we find the Ten Commandments. In reality, we find commands from God throughout the Bible. The word "let" here means *"do"* and implies that it's something He expects us *to utilize* on a regular basis. This Light He's talking about is not something that is of us, but rather, it's of Jesus and because He's put the Light in us, He wants us to do something with it.

So how do we Turn On The Light? We do so in the following manner:

- We are to love people as Christ has commanded us to do. He gave us this commandment in John 15:12 whereby He said, *"This is my commandment, that ye love one another, as I have loved you."*

- We are to have compassion on people even as Christ has compassion on us. The Bible teaches us in Mark 6:34, *"And Jesus, when he came out, saw much people, and was moved with compassion toward them, because they were as sheep not having a shepherd: and he began to teach them many things."* We see people all the time who appear to have no hope and the Lord wants us to have compassion on them. It's then that we Turn On The Light!

- We are to intercede for people as Christ interceded for us. Prayer is always in order and as we pray for people and God sends forth

His blessings we are letting our Light shine. Some people have no faith, no hope, and are blinded to the truth of God; but if and when, we begin to intercede for them, the scales can be removed from their eyes. The Apostle Paul said in 2 Corinthians 4:3-4, *"But if our gospel be hid, it is hid to them that are lost: In whom the god of this world hath blinded the minds of them which believe not, lest the light of the glorious gospel of Christ, who is the image of God, should shine unto them."*

It's not ours to keep to ourselves, – it's time to Turn On The Light!!!

We're Told That Others May See It

In giving us the command to let your Light so shine, the Lord also tells us how – *"before men, that they may see your good works."* Just like you can't hide natural light, neither can we hide the light that's within us. When we are seen doing what's required of us, others will acknowledge our efforts. You see, you're not required to Turn On The Light just so you can see what's happening – it's so others can see what the Lord is doing through you!

- Somebody needs to see God working through you

- Somebody needs to see your Faith in action

- Somebody needs to see you Plead the Blood of Jesus over your life, your marriage, your home, your job, your children, your situation, and see the Power of God show up in His time

- Somebody needs to hear you say, *"it might be bad right now, but …greater is he that is in you, than he that is in the world!"* (1 John 4:4)

Jesus gave us the greatest example of what this looks like when He went from judgment hall to judgment hall, yet He continued to let His Light shine. Even while yet hanging on the cross, He continued to commune with His Heavenly Father, yet taking care of the sins of the world, when He eventually gave up the Ghost and died, Matthew tells us that there was a great earthquake and a centurion who was with Jesus throughout His crucifixion said in Matthew 27:54, *"Truly this was the Son of God."* A statement like that can only be said if you Turn On The Light!!!

We're Told That God Will Get the Glory

Verse 16 further goes on to say, *"...and glorify your Father which is in heaven."* The Preacher's Outline and Sermon Bible makes a very interesting statement here which says, *"Believers are to let their light shine to stir men to glorify God. This is the supreme reason why our light is to shine before men: to stir them to glorify God. The glory of God is to be the primary aim of all believers."*[15] This is further amplified in 1 Peter 4:11 which reads, *"If any man speak, let him speak as the oracles of God; if any man minister, let him do it as of the ability which God giveth: that God in all things may be glorified through Jesus Christ, to whom be praise and dominion for ever and ever."* Everything we do should be for the Glory of God:

- How we behave before men
- How we behave when people aren't watching
- How we behave at home
- How we behave on the job
- How we behave in worship
- How we behave on vacation
- How we behave during business transactions
- How we behave before non-believers

Our very existence should be for God's Glory! We do so because we are not our own. Paul said in 1 Corinthians 6:20, *"For ye are bought with a price: therefore glorify God in your body, and in your spirit, which are God's."*

I need to spend a few minutes talking about the source of our Light which is found in the Gospel of John. In John 1:3-5, *"All things were made by him; and without him was not any thing made that was made. 4 In him was life; and the life was the light of men. 5 And the light shineth in darkness; and the darkness comprehended it not."* John further went on to say in John 1:9, *"That was the true Light, which lighteth every man*

---

[15] Ibid, page 71

Turn On The Light!

that cometh into the world." John was talking about the True Light of the world and if we're going to Turn On the Light, we've got to know *who* the True Light is for ourselves.

- He Came down through 40 and two generations
- He Healed the sick, Raised the dead and gave sight to the blind
- He was Crucified on Calvary's Cross
- He hung, bled, and died for your sins and mine
- He got up early on Sunday morning with all Power in His hands

I said earlier that when Jesus said, *"Let your light so shine…"* it was not a suggestion! What are you going to do now that you know what the Lord requires? I can't speak for you, but I've turned on my light a long time ago and I'm going to keep it on!!!

"This little light of mine, I'm gonna let it shine;

Everywhere I go, I'm gonna let it shine;

All in my home, I'm gonna let it shine;

Jesus gave it to me, and I'm gonna let it shine;

Let it shine, let it shine, let it shine!"

Principles of Kingdom Living

Principles of
KINGDOM LIVING
How to Live Right in a World Gone Wrong

CHAPTER
6

JESUS AND THE LAW

"Think not that I am come to destroy the law, or the prophets: I am not come to destroy, but to fulfill. For verily I say unto you, Till heaven and earth pass, one jot or one tittle shall in no wise pass from the law, till all be fulfilled."

Matthew 5:17-18

Our society is governed by a set of laws that are in place to keep "good order and discipline." From a national or political perspective, we have elected officials who are referred to as "lawmakers" and their responsibility is to ensure laws are established for the betterment of society. From a Spiritual perspective, we have Moses the "lawgiver" who was used by God to present the laws to the people.

Principles of Kingdom Living

It was God Himself who established laws for mankind and made them initially available to us in Exodus 20, which is where we find the 10 Commandments. I will go on record again and say that they are not the 10 Recommendations or the 10 Suggestions, but are commands from God, Who is the Creator of everything. For the most part, people abide by the laws of the land and because of that, they don't have to worry about looking over their shoulders, waiting for the police or whomever to come and take them away.

I think it's important for us to understand that when it comes to the Bible, the New Testament reveals what the Old Testament conceals. Jesus came to be a fulfillment of the law and the prophets and take care of the requirements for salvation. Because of His unique approach to the law and the gospel, many people accused Him of destroying the law of God. What they didn't understand was that His purpose was to set the record straight and take the necessary steps to make sure the law was fulfilled just as the Scriptures said it would be.

People had a problem with Jesus because He was making sure the law was followed as established. There's nothing new under the sun as we're living in a day and time when people want to do things their own way and push aside the laws of God and the land. It's interesting to me that most of the laws in our penal code have their foundation in the 10 Commandments. God's Laws are Right, God's Laws Are Fair, and God's Laws Are Needed for our society. If His Laws are not followed, chaos, confusion, and rebellion will begin to be the norm in the land.

> - We have chaos in our society right now with the recent verdict in the Trayvon Martin trial whereby people have started riots, looting, and destroying property.
> - We have confusion in our society right now with the recent decision of the Supreme Court of the United States with regards to same-sex marriage.
> - We have rebellion in our society right now with laws on the books that people blatantly break on a daily basis.

In the natural, when we break the law and are caught, we are held accountable for that law; when it comes to God's Law, we are also held accountable for breaking it. The key to it all is to know what the law is and do your very best to abide by God's Law! Jesus knew the law and showed us how to abide by the law.

In our selected text, Jesus is dealing with the fact that some have accused Him of trying to destroy what God has established. People have a tendency of doing things like that when their intent is to do what they want to do, regardless of the established laws. *The Preacher's Outline and Sermon Bible* writes, *"Every generation has its proponents who feel that Jesus emphasized love and de-emphasized the law. Many have felt that the thrust of Jesus is love and forgiveness, and the afterthought is law and justice. As a result, many have felt less obligated to follow God's Law. They have felt freer to live a looser life and to do as they wished."*[16] They further go on to say, "Therefore, the law's clear restrictions and obligations and its demand for obedience are minimized, and what is called love and forgiveness is emphasized." [17] We can see that in the fact that people have said the government does not have the right to tell somebody who to love. Jesus told us, *"to love our neighbor as ourselves,"* but did not tell us to love them with the same love that we have for our spouses. There is a difference!

I want to focus on the fact that Jesus is the epitome of keeping the law and the prophets and lived a life reflective of that.

<u>Jesus Fulfilled the Law</u>

The law was established to teach mankind how to live a holy and righteous life. Because sin had entered the world, the law had to be established to provide us with guidelines to live by. The Bible teaches us in Romans 3:23, *"For all have sinned and come short of the glory of God."* Some say that the Law was impossible to keep, but Jesus showed us that it was possible to do so. Too many times we want to hide behind our humanity in order to do what we want to do, but if we really took a look at ourselves, we will find that we are Spirit Beings, made in the image and likeness of God. John 4:24 says, *"God is a spirit, and they that worship him must worship him in spirit and in truth."* Jesus embraced the law, put His flesh in subjection and lived a sinless life. 1 Peter 2:21-24 says, *"For even hereunto were ye called: because Christ also suffered for us, leaving us an example, that we should follow his*

[16]Ibid, page 72
[17]Ibid, page 72

steps: 22 Who did no sin, neither was guile found in his mouth: 23 Who, when he was reviled, reviled not again; when he suffered, he threathened not; but committed himself to him that judgeth righteously: 24 Who his own self bare our sins in his own body on the tree, that we, being dead to sins, should live unto righteousness: by whose stripes ye were healed." Jesus fulfilled the law!!

Jesus Fulfilled the Prophets

God had to bring in the savior in such a way that man could not take credit for it. When He created man, He formed man from the dust of the earth, and breathed into him that he became a living soul. Now with the Messiah, He had to do something that would confirm the identity of the Messiah. It was prophesied that the Messiah would be born supernaturally! In Isaiah 7:14 we find, *"Therefore the Lord himself shall give you a sign; Behold, a virgin shall conceive, and bear a son, and shall call his name Immanuel."* This was fulfilled in Matthew 1:18 which reads, *"Now the birth of Jesus Christ was on this wise: When his mother Mary was espoused to Joseph, before they came together, she was found with child of the Holy Ghost."*

The prophet Micah prophesied where Christ would be born. He foretells in Micah 5:2, *"But thou, Bethlehem Ephratah, though thou be little among the thousands of Judah, yet out of thee shall he come forth unto me that is to be ruler in Israel; whose going forth have been from of old, from everlasting."* This was fulfilled in Matthew 2:1-2 which says, *"Now when Jesus was born in Bethlehem of Judea in the days of Herod the king, behold, there came wise men from the east to Jerusalem, 2 Saying, Where is he that is born King of the Jews? for we have seen his star in the east, and are come to worship him."*

The Bible also teaches us that the Messiah would suffer for the sake of mankind. Again, we find in Isaiah 53:4-5, *"Surely he hath borne our griefs, and carried our sorrows: yet we did esteem him stricken, smitten of God, and afflicted. 5 But he was wounded for our transgressions, he was bruised for our iniquities: the chastisement of our peace was upon him; and with his stripes we are healed."* This was fulfilled in John 19:1 which reads, *"Then Pilate therefore took Jesus and scourged him."* The word "scourged" in this verse comes from a Greek word which means to whip, or to lash as a public punishment. Jesus fulfilled the prophets!!!

Jesus And The Law

Jesus Will Fulfill The Word

In verse 18, Jesus says, *"Till heaven and earth pass, one jot or one tittle shall in no wise pass from the law, till all be fulfilled."* A jot is the smallest letter in the Hebrew language and a tittle is the smallest ornament placed upon certain Hebrew letters. If you leave out a "jot" or a "tittle," you change the meaning and impact of the word or phrase. For example, if you take the apostrophe out of the letters G-O-D-S, now you have multiple Gods instead of something that belongs to God. What Jesus is telling us is that whatever God has put in place will happen, and whatever Jesus has promised will come to pass. I'm reminded of what Jesus said in John 2:19 where He said, *"Destroy this temple, and in three days I will raise it up."* When He made this statement, He was not talking about a building, but rather His body in death. The Apostle Paul verifies this in 1 Corinthians 15:3-4 which reads, *"For I delivered unto you first of all that which I also received, how that Christ died for our sins according to the scriptures: 4 And that he was buried, and that he rose again the third day according to the scriptures."* But Jesus also made a promise that we can all look forward to when He said in John 14:2-3, *"In my Father's house are many mansions: if it were not so, I would have told you. I go to prepare a place for you. 3 And if I go to prepare a place for you, I will come again, and receive you unto myself, that where I am, there ye may be also."*

I said all that to say we may not agree with how the law or justice is rendered here in America but we have One that we can turn to who is the Righteous Judge and King who will rule appropriately and fairly. We don't have to be upset behind His ruling, because His ruling will be right! He's Jesus Christ and He can't make a mistake; He's Jesus Christ and He can't make a bad decision; He's Jesus Christ and He will fulfill all righteousness!

- We needed a Savior, and He Came on the scene!
- We needed a Deliverer, and He Came on the scene!
- We needed a Healer, and He Came on the scene!
- We needed a Provider, and He Came on the scene!
- We needed a Protector, and He Came on the scene!

Principles of Kingdom Living

- We needed a Shepherd, and He Came on the scene!
- He's Jesus the Christ, King of kings and Lord of lords!
- He was Crucified for your sins and mine!
- He was Buried for your sins and mine!
- He Rose early on Sunday morning, with all Power in His hands for your sins and mine!
- He's Coming back one day as King and Judge!!!

Principles of
KINGDOM LIVING
How to Live Right in a World Gone Wrong

CHAPTER

7

"GET YOUR RIGHTEOUSNESS RIGHT!!"

"Whosoever therefore shall break one of these least commandments, and shall teach men so, he shall be called the least in the Kingdom of Heaven: but whosoever shall do and teach them, the same shall be called great in the Kingdom of Heaven. For I say unto you, That except your righteousness shall exceed the righteousness of the scribes and Pharisees, ye shall in no case enter into the Kingdom of Heaven."

Matthew 5:19-20

When you think about the words righteous or righteousness, one of the first thoughts that comes to mind is being and doing things correctly. The

Principles of Kingdom Living

American Heritage Dictionary defines the word righteous (the root word for righteousness) as being "morally upright or just." When you examine the word righteousness from the text in the original Greek you find that it's defined as "equity (the state of being just, impartial, and fair) of character or act, specifically Christian."

One of the problems in our society today is that, generally speaking, people don't have any morals anymore. Because we've bought into the mindset and idea that, "it's all about me; I can do want I want to do; you don't have the right to tell me what I'm supposed to be doing; and you do what you want to do and I'll do what I want to do." I don't know if you caught it, but the word "I" seemed to be the focal point of each of those statements.

A few examples of this can be found in recent headlines;

> - Former U. S. Representative Anthony Weiner was accused and admitted to sending inappropriate pictures and text messages to upwards of 10 women, yet he still wanted to be the mayor of New York City,
> - In Cleveland, OH, Ariel Castro kidnapped and raped three women over a period of 10 years, caused one of them to miscarry several pregnancies, but blames everything on his so-called addiction,
> - In San Diego, former Mayor Bob Filner had been accused of inappropriate behavior against women and staff personnel; admitted his behavior was not appropriate; decided to admit himself into an "intensive" two-week therapy/rehab program, in an effort to correct many years of inappropriate behavior, yet he was very reluctant to resign from office.

What I see in all of these cases are acts of selfishness with no real regard for others or how their actions may affect other people. When I look at our selected text, I find that Jesus is trying to get us to take a very good, close, and hard look at ourselves to see if we are conducting ourselves in a manner that is pleasing and acceptable to God. Now let's understand something here, our righteousness, according to Isaiah 64:6 says, *"But we are all as an unclean thing, and all our righteousnesses are as filthy rags; and*

Get Your Righteousness Right!!

we all do fade as a leaf; and our iniquities, like the wind, have taken us away." Our righteousness makes a turn for the better when we accept Christ as Lord and savior and take on His righteousness. This then gives us a moral compass and gives us direction on how to live a righteous life. What am I trying to say? If you don't know Jesus, **Get Your Righteousness Right!** If you do know Jesus but want to do your own thing and not operate in obedience to His Will and Word, **Get Your Righteousness Right!**

Jesus starts off in verse 19 talking about breaking the least of the commandments. What was He referring to here? God gave us 10 Commandments in Exodus 20 which were His requirements for living a righteous and holy life. The Rabbis and religious leaders took those same 10 and turned them into 613, which made it extremely difficult to keep and abide by. One of the things they also did was assert that some of the commandments were weightier than others, but that's not how God see's it. Here's my point: with God, sin is sin is sin, and none carries more weight than others. For example, a lie carries the same weight as murder in the sight of God, because with Him, sin is sin is sin! The problem is that people were justifying their actions, calling them acceptable, and teaching others that it's alright to do those things. In today's society, we have the tendency of saying, "well, I can't do everything that needs to be done…but God knows my heart!" The reality of it all is that He does know our hearts and knows when we can do better, or when we're doing the bare minimum, or don't want to do better!! God is not looking for excuses; He's looking for obedience, especially from those who are called the Household of Faith!

We should never shirk our responsibility to teach others how to live righteously because the Scriptures teach us in Luke 12:48b, *"For unto whomsoever much is given, of him shall be much required: and to whom men have committed much, of him they will ask the more."* We have the responsibility to share with others what we have learned regarding eternal life. I've said before that this gospel we have will do us no real good if we keep it to ourselves. It's a give-a-way gospel and the more we do so, the more the Lord will replenish it in our lives.

The Lord further goes on to deal with the Kingdom of Heaven. This is the kingdom that will be established when He returns as King of kings and

Lord of lords. Christ Will Come and set up His literal Earthly Kingdom that will last forever. My question before you today is…do you want to be counted as least or great in the Kingdom of Heaven?

So let's take a few minutes to talk about **Get Your Righteousness Right!!**

We Can't Be Religious

The Pharisees were so focused on keeping the letter of the Law, that they missed the Spirit of the Law. Their keeping of the Law actually put people in bondage rather than setting people free. What they wanted more than anything else is to be seen of men doing acts of righteousness, but it was only for their individual benefit, and not the Kingdom's Glory. *The Preacher's Outline and Sermon Bible* says here, *"The religionist, the Pharisees and the Scribes, had some righteousness. They just did not have enough. They were, in fact, strict religionists. They worked at obeying thousands and thousands of rules and regulations, governing everything ranging from dress and social behavior to ministry and work. However, they lacked the one essential: loving God so much that they would deny themselves and seek their righteousness in His Son, Jesus Christ."*[18] They looked the part, they talked the part; they gave the impression they were living the part, but they missed the mark by focusing on themselves and not on God. Even in our society today, there are some who feel that going to worship Sunday after Sunday is being obedient to God. Here's the problem; we can go to worship, or do many things religiously, but when we arrive, are we really fulfilling the Spirit of the Law? We are made to give God Glory and evidence of this is found in Isaiah 43:7 which says, *"Even every one that is called by my name: for I have created him for my glory, I have formed him; yea, I have made him."* We're taught that God is looking for true worshippers! In John 4:24 we find, *"God is a spirit: and they that worship him must worship him in spirit and in truth."* We can't be religious as the Pharisees were and therefore, when we break the threshold of the House of the Lord, our minds should be made up to give God the Glory that is Due His Name, because God knows our hearts!!

We Must Live Righteous

This has a lot to do with not just what people see of us, but more

[18]Ibid, page 76

Get Your Righteousness Right!!

importantly, what God sees when nobody else is watching! You see, it's easy to live righteous in front of people – go about doing good; helping people; being seen doing acts of kindness; saying the right things at the right time – but what about your motives? God never intended that we give the impression of being good or righteous, but expected us to live it daily. Again, *The Preacher's Outline and Sermon Bible* says, *"Some feel they must do good to be acceptable to God. Their motive in life is to work and work at doing good in order to secure God's acceptance. They have never learned the truth: they cannot do enough good to be perfectly acceptable to God. They must trust His love – that He loves them so much that He will take their trust and count it as righteousness."*[19] When we think about this quote, we must come to the understanding that we cannot work for our salvation because the Bible teaches us in Ephesians 2:8-9, *"For by grace are ye saved through faith; and that not of yourselves: it is the gift of God: not of works, lest any man should boast."*

So how do we live righteous? Well, let's see what the Bible has to say about that…

- We've got to know God! In Exodus 3:6 we find, *"Moreover he said, I am the God of thy father, the God of Abraham, the God of Isaac, and the God of Jacob."*
- We've got to know God's Word. In Joshua 1:8 we find, *"This book of the Law shall not depart out of thy mouth; but thou shalt meditate therein day and night, that thou mayest observe to do according to all that is written therein: for then thou shalt make thy way prosperous, and then thou shalt have good success."*
- We've got to know how to worship God. In Psalm 9:1-2 we find, *"I will praise thee, O Lord, with my whole heart; I will shew forth all thy marvelous works."*
- We've got to love God. In Psalm 18:1 we find, *"I will love thee, O Lord, my strength."*
- We've got to trust God. In Psalm 71:1 we find, *"In thee, O Lord, do I put my trust: let me never be put to confusion."*

[19] Ibid, page 77

Principles of Kingdom Living

- We've got to love one another. Jesus said in Mark 12:31, *"And the second is like, namely this, Thou shalt love thy neighbor as thyself. There is none other commandment than these."*

So if we want to get our righteousness right, we've got to get right with Jesus! He's the end all as it pertains to righteousness. Romans 10:4 tells us, *"For Christ is the end of the law for righteousness to everyone that believeth."* Paul makes that statement because Christ is the One from whom we can receive our righteousness! Let me tell you what righteousness did for us!

- Righteousness put on human flesh
- Righteousness came down through 40 and two Generations
- Righteousness was born of a virgin
- Righteousness was found in a manger
- Righteousness Consulted with the religious leaders with great knowledge at a very young age
- Righteousness Healed a blind man
- Righteousness Healed a man with a withered hand
- Righteousness was betrayed by a kiss
- Righteousness was falsely accused
- Righteousness was condemned to die
- Righteousness was placed on a cross
- Righteousness was pierced in the side
- Righteousness Died on a cross
- Righteousness was placed in a borrowed tomb
- Righteousness got up early Sunday morning…

Principles of
KINGDOM LIVING
How to Live Right in a World Gone Wrong

CHAPTER 8

GET YOUR RELATIONSHIPS RIGHT
PART I

"Ye have heard that it was said by them of old time, Thou shalt not kill; and whosoever shall kill shall be in danger of the judgment: But I say unto you, that whosoever is angry with his brother without a cause shall be in danger of the judgment: and whosoever shall say to his brother Raca, shall be in danger of the council: but whosoever shall say, Thou fool, shall be in danger of hell fire. Therefore if thou bring thy gift to the altar, and there rememberest that thy brother hath ought against thee: Leave there thy gift before the altar, and go thy way; first be reconciled to thy brother, and then come and offer thy gift. Agree with thine adversary *quickly, whiles thou art in the way with him; lest at any time the adversary deliver thee to the judge, and the judge deliver thee to the officer, and thou be cast into prison. Verily I say unto thee, Thou shalt by no means come out thence, till thou hast paid the uttermost farthing."*

Matthew 5:21-26

When God created man, He did it so that man could have a relationship with Him and both with each other. God was not lonely when He created man, but He did want His creation to worship and praise Him. In order for us to do so, we must have a relationship with Him.

God is not looking for us to be religious when it comes to Him, but He does want us to be in relationship with Him. Have you noticed that it's a lot easier to deal with people when your relationship with them is going well?

> You can talk to them about anything and everything

> You can hang out with them and not have to worry about what they are thinking about you

> You don't have to worry about avoiding them when you see them but you can spend quality time building that relationship

NEWSFLASH!! Most times, we avoid God because our relationship with Him is not right or current! Because sometimes we're not doing everything to build our relationship with Him, it becomes difficult to deal with God. I have learned and am learning that God loves us so much that He will patiently wait for us to come back to Him to get things right with Him. I'm reminded of the parable that Jesus shares in Luke 15 about the prodigal son. We must understand that a parable is an earthly story with a heavenly message, so Jesus uses things of this world to help us to understand the heavenly message. In this parable, a son goes to his father and asks for his inheritance, before the father dies. The father agrees and the son leaves home and blows all his money. He gets to the point that he spends all of his inheritance on fast living, thus finding himself eating with the pigs. He realizes that his father has much wealth and many servants and decides

Get Your Relationships Right, Part I

to go back home to his father and become one of his servants. When the father sees the son a great distance off, he runs to meet him because he was so happy to see him. Although the son hurt the father in leaving, the father receives him not as a servant, but as a son and restores the relationship with him.

That's how God wants to deal with us!!! He's ready to restore us as His children, but we've got to take the steps to restore the Relationship!! Today, we want to deal with the topic, "Get Your Relationship Right!!!

In our selected text, Jesus is continuing His exposition of the Sermon on the Mount and sharing with those in attendance, truths that effects and impacts their lives on a daily basis. One thing can be said about the Word of God is that it transcends time and is just as applicable today as it was when it was being written. Here the Lord is dealing with a few things that were pertinent then and are still pertinent now. Let's deal with them as well.

If you are going to Get Your Relationships Right, you must:

Be Careful How We Handle People (verses 21-22)

In these verses, Jesus is dealing with the topic of murder, which is the taking of one's life. If we were to closely take inventory of this we would come to the conclusion that we don't have the power to give life and therefore we don't have the power to take it either. When He said in verse 21, *"Ye have heard it said by them of old time, Thou shalt not kill; and whosoever shall kill shall be in danger of the judgment,"* He was making reference to Exodus 20:13 and Deuteronomy 5:17 which both read, *"Thou shalt not kill."* This word "kill" in our selected text means to murder, slay, or in other words, take another's life. I have found that we don't normally kill people by taking their lives, but we do have the power to kill people by killing their goals–killing their dreams–or killing their Spiritual Growth! Here's what I'm getting at: people join a local Church and want to get involved but the people who are already involved don't look too kindly on newcomers because of the way they dress, because they don't know much about the Lord, or because of their background. Too many times, we only want to be around people who are just like us and so we'll push them away because of our perceptions of them! Or when they do get involved and because we don't have a solid understanding of the Word, we try to get them to take on our idea of what's being taught and have the Word compromised to fit society, instead of having society to fit the Word of God! Let me be very clear and real here…God has not changed; His Word has not changed and He and it will never change! I know society is changing but society needs to change to the Word of God. That's why the Apostle Paul said in Romans 12:2, *"And be not conformed to this world, but be ye transformed by the renewing of your minds, that ye may prove what is that good, and acceptable, and perfect will of God."*

In being careful on how we deal with people, we have to be careful as to what we say to them. In verse 22, Jesus uses the word Raca, an old Aramaic word that's only used this one time in Scripture. *Strong's Exhaustive Concordance of the Bible* defines the word Raca as, *"O empty one, i.e. thou worthless (as a term of utter vilification)."*[20] Who wants to be called worthless or empty? Not me for sure, and I'm confident you feel the same way. Therefore, we should be mindful of what King Solomon shares with us in Proverbs 15:1 which reads, *"A soft answer turneth away wrath: but grievous words stir up anger."*

Be Careful How We Deal With Each Other (verses 23-24)

Right here the Lord begins to get deep on us! He's dealing with the fact that we can't rightfully bring a sincere gift to Him if we have issues with one another. The word "gift" in this text comes from the Greek word "doron" and literally means *"a present; specifically a sacrifice: - gift, offering"*[21] and He's telling us we can't bring it to Him in good standing if we have problems with each other. I said in the previous chapter that sometimes we do things that are not quite up to the Lord's standards and will give the excuse, "but the Lord knows my heart." Guess what, He knows if your heart is not right when it comes to how we deal with each other!! Say *"Amen"* or *"Ouch,"* you know which one applies to you!!!

One of the things the Lord is dealing with here is reconciliation, which means, "to reestablish a close relationship between; to settle or resolve." According to the *Preacher's Outline and Sermon Bible*, there are at least four reasons why this is so important:

[20] Strong's Exhaustive Concordance of the Bible, Updated Edition
[21] Ibid

Get Your Relationships Right, Part I

1. *"Reconciliation with God is one of the major purposes of worship. A person worships in order to seek reconciliation and fellowship with God and His people. Therefore, God does not accept the worship of a person who holds malice against Him or any of His people.*

2. *A person is to worship, for worship is essential to life and eternity. But worship is unacceptable to God unless a person is reconciled with his brothers.*

3. *Bad feelings between believers hinder worship. Worship is meaningless unless a person is right with his brother. Reconciliation must always precede worship.*

4. *Worship is a time for a person to reflect and to examine his heart and life to see if there is 'any wicked way' within him. It is essential that he search his heart. Worship is not acceptable if bad or wicked feelings against others are within the human heart."* [22]

The bottom line is that you and I cannot come into the house of the Lord to Worship Him In Spirit and In Truth if we have a lot of unresolved issues with our brothers and sisters! The Bible teaches us in 1 John 4:20-21, *"If a man say, I love God, and hateth his brother, he is a liar: for he that loveth not his brother whom he hath seen, how can he love God whom he hath not seen? 21 And this commandment have we from him, That he who loveth God love his brother also."* That's why the Apostle Paul shares with us in Ephesians 4:31-32, *"Let all bitterness, and wrath, and anger, and clamour, and evil speaking, be put away from you, with all malice: and be ye kind one to another, tenderhearted, forgiving one another, even as God for Christ's sake hath forgiven you."* We've got to learn how to love one another, get along with one another, deal with what needs to be dealt with, and leave the past in the past!!! Stop letting the devil bring up old news and start sharing the Good News concerning Jesus Christ!!! We've got to make sure we do what's right; make sure things are right with each other; so we can give Christ what's right!!!

---

[22] Preacher's Outline and Sermon Bible, Matthew 1, page 81

Principles of Kingdom Living

Be Careful How We Deal With Our Adversaries (verse 25-26)

I think the first thing we need to do here is identify who our adversary is. By definition, an adversary is "an opponent or an enemy." Here in the text, Jesus says, *"Agree with thine adversary quickly..."* Let me be very clear here, Jesus is not saying to give in or compromise with your adversary, especially as it pertains to what's contrary to the Word of God. What He's saying is to work out something that will be mutually agreeable between the two parties. There may come a time when you will have to say, "let us agree to disagree" and that's alright if you are standing on the Word of God. I said earlier that times have changed, but the Word of God has not changed; therefore, we should not be compelled to compromise when it comes to His word!!

The context of this text has to do with civil suits between two parties and how they can have an impact on each, and especially on the testimony of the Christian. Christ is saying that we should do our best to resolve our issues before they have a negative impact on our walk. People will talk, and people will talk, and by the way, people will talk, especially if a Christian is found tied up in court about something that could have been resolved outside of a courtroom. Again, *The Preacher's Outline and Sermon Bible* says there are at least two reasons why it's dangerous to hold on to anger:

1. *"There is an earthly danger. Barriers can lead to serious action ranging from legal suits to imprisonment. Such action is tragic to God and among God's people. It is even forbidden among Christian brothers as found in 1 Corinthians 6:1-8.*

2. *There is an eternal danger. Life does not last and the day of final judgment is coming. A person's judgment for holding a grudge against a brother will be severe."*[23]

Jesus teaches us how to deal with our adversary in Matthew 4 when the Holy Spirit sent Him out to the desert to be tempted by the devil. Every time the devil came at Him, Jesus took him to the Word of God. On three occasions, Jesus said, *"It is written"* and each time He said it, the devil had to back down. In order for us to be able to effectively say, *"It is written,"* we have to know WHAT is written! The devil is going to come after you, but

---

[23]Ibid, page 82

Get Your Relationships Right, Part I

you've got to handle him just the way Jesus did!

So if you want to get all these relationships right, you've got to get the main relationship right, and that's a relationship with Jesus Christ!

We have to accept the fact that it was Jesus who hung, bled, and died on a hill called Calvary.

We have to accept the fact that it was Jesus who rose early on Sunday morning with all power in His hands!!

When we have a relationship with Him, it enables us to handle people the right way; it enables us to deal with one another the right way; and it enables us to deal with our adversaries!!

If you know Jesus, you can know peace–but if you don't know Jesus, there will be no peace!!!

Principles of Kingdom Living

Principles of
KINGDOM LIVING
How to Live Right in a World Gone Wrong

CHAPTER
9

GET YOUR RELATIONSHIPS RIGHT, PART II

"Ye have heard that it was said by them of old time, Thou shalt not commit adultery: But I say unto you, That whosoever looketh on a woman to lust after her hath committed adultery with her already in his heart. And if thy right eye offend thee, pluck it out, and cast it from thee: for it is profitable for thee that one of thy members should perish, and not that thy whole body should be cast into hell. And if thy right hand offend thee, cut it off, and cast it from thee: for it is profitable for thee that one of thy members should perish, and not that thy whole body should be cast into hell. It hath been said, Whosoever shall put away his wife, let him give her a writing of divorcement: But I

say unto you, That whosoever shall put away his wife, saving for the cause of fornication, causeth her to commit adultery: and whosoever shall marry her that is divorced committeth adultery.

Matthew 5:27-32

As I've stated before, God created us to worship Him, and have relationships with one another.

Marriage was instituted by God to be a physical reflection of our spiritual relationship with Him, and anybody who wants to divorce God, in my opinion, needs to get checked out!!

> It was God who Created the Institution of Marriage between one man and one woman as evidenced in the Book of Genesis

> It was God who intended that the Relationship be monogamous and not have any outside influences and distractions

> It was God who never intended for divorce to be something that takes place with regard to those Relationships

Concerning this Relationship between one man and one woman, I believe society has conditioned us to believe (1) that intimacy is a bad thing due to the entertainment industry – namely magazines, movies, and even some shows on prime time television; and (2) that you don't need to remain faithful to your spouse or even your friend. Somebody once said, *"The grass is always greener on the other side"* but I have found out that the grass that is greener is the one you water or nurture, so if you want it to be green, you've got to work on it!!!

Intimacy is a very important part of the marriage relationship and God addresses it in His word. I think sometimes people forget that God created intimacy and since He did, He also gave instructions as to how it should be carried out. When done God's way, it's a beautiful expression of love between two people; but when it's done society's way, it can bring about trouble in the marriage and in the home. I've said before that what's present with us is actually history with God as He knows the end from the beginning, so He knew there would be some problems when it comes to intimacy. It's no coincidence He makes it plain for us in the 10 Commandments, which is actually for our own good!

Here in our selected text, Jesus is still sharing His Sermon on the Mount and dealing with relationships. In Part I, He dealt with three other relationships; (1) Other People; (2) One Another; and (3) Our Adversaries. Now He begins to deal with relationships between a man and a woman and how the religious leaders, or society, have twisted what God intended.

There are two things that Jesus is dealing with here, adultery, which is sex outside of the marriage relationship, and divorce, which ends the marriage.

I'd like to give us some practical things we can do to get and keep our relationships right – before men and before God.

If you are going to Get Your Relationships Right:

Make A Covenant With Your Eyes (verse 27-28)

As Jesus was explaining and defining this text, He was dealing with the fact that the act of adultery does not always take place physically, but it starts in the heart. He took them back to Exodus 20:14 which reads, *"Thou shalt not commit adultery."* Isn't it interesting that society has called it an "affair" but God called it "adultery." If we change the name of it, it might not hurt us so bad, but it's all adultery with God! Jesus goes beyond the physical act of adultery and starts to deal with the eyes and the heart! He said in verse 28, *"whosoever looketh on a woman to lust after her hath committed adultery with her already in his heart."* Before I go any further, I think I need to clarify something for all of us. What Jesus is sharing us with us is a principle which means, it's applicable for both the man and the woman. There are some men and women alike that lust after the opposite sex, and unfortunately, in the society we now live in, openly lust after the same sex! With God, sin is sin is sin regardless of which gender is doing it!!

The word lust in this text comes from the Greek word *'epithymeo'* and it means *to set the heart upon; to long for; covet, desire.*[24] It's through the eyes that this takes place because the eyes are the gateway to the heart and the soul.

You see, not everybody is upright, saved, sanctified, and filled with the Holy

[24]Strong's Exhaustive Concordance of the Bible, Updated Edition

Ghost. There are people out there who want you to look at them in that manner just so they can have their way. We're living in a day and time when both men and women are wearing their clothes too tight, men wearing what I call "smediums" which means it's the size between a small and a medium, and definitely too tight for them; and women are doing the same, or wearing hardly nothing at all. Shorts so short they shouldn't be called shorts; shirts that are too revealing and almost expose everything. It's because of these actions that we need to make a covenant with our eyes!!!

Solomon said in Proverbs 6:25, *"Lust not after her beauty in thine heart; neither let her take thee with her eyelids."* The Preacher's Outline and Sermon Bible says here, *"There is real danger in using one's eyes sinfully. Peter warns that a person can lose control: [2 Peter 2:14] "Having eyes full of adultery, and that cannot cease from sin; beguiling unstable souls: an heart they have exercised with covetous practices; cursed children…"* If we are going to get it right, we should probably follow the example of Job when he said in Job 31:1, *"I made a covenant with my eyes; why then should I think upon a maid?"* And when we make that covenant with our eyes, we allow God to guide our actions.

Make A Covenant With Your Body (verse 29-30)

It's interesting to me that Jesus went from the function of the eyes to getting rid of the eyes AND the hands. The question was asked, "Why did Christ use the eyes and hands to illustrate His point?" The answer provided was, "because a man is moved primarily by thoughts that arise from sight, and a woman is moved primarily by touch."[25] You see, Jesus is dealing with this from the point that both men and women are effected by this. We must remember that our bodies are temples and the place where God dwells. The Apostle Paul reminds us of this in 1 Corinthians 3:16-17 which says, *"Know ye not that ye are the temple of God, and that the Spirit of God dwelleth in you? 17 If any man defile the temple of God, him shall God destroy; for the temple of God is holy, which temple you are."* Then he goes on further to stress this point in 1 Corinthians 6:19 which reads, *"What? Know ye not that your body is the temple of the Holy Ghost which is in you, which ye have of God, and ye are not your own?"* When we make a covenant with our bodies we understand that they're not ours in the first place, but

[25] Anonymous

Get Your Relationships Right, Part II

we should handle our body in a manner that's pleasing unto God.

Make A Covenant With God (verse 31-32)

When it comes to marriage nowadays, society says that one out of every two will end in divorce. Some people enter into marriage with the idea that they take a "trial run" and if it doesn't work out, they can get out of it and try again. That's not what God intended from the beginning. Jesus here deals with what was shared in Deuteronomy 24:1 which reads, *"When a man hath taken a wife, and married her, and it comes to pass that she find no favour in his eyes, because he hath found some uncleanness in her: then let him write her a bill of divorcement, and give it in her hand, and send her out of his house."* In Old Testament days, there were many reasons as to why a man could divorce his wife, but God never intended for divorce to be part of daily life. Now the Lord gives a specific reason for divorce and it's referred to as "fornication" in Verse 32, which is actually adultery. Now let's be clear here, Malachi 2:16 in the King James Version says, *"For the Lord, the God of Israel, saith that he hateth putting away: for one covereth violence with his garment, saith the Lord of hosts: therefore take heed to your spirit, that ye deal not treacherously."* But in the Amplified Bible it reads, *"For the Lord, the God of Israel, says: I hate divorce and marital separation, and him who covers his garment [his wife] with violence. Therefore keep a watch upon your spirit [that it may be controlled by My Spirit], that you deal not treacherously and faithlessly [with your marriage mate.]"*[26] In other words, God hates divorce and that was not His original intention when He instituted marriage. Jesus further explains that if the marriage is going in the direction of divorce, to be in a right standing with God, adultery or fornication is the only acceptable reason for divorce.

God has promised to deal with those who commit adultery and many other actions against the will of God. He's told us in 1 Corinthians 6:9-10, *"Know ye not that the unrighteous shall not inherit the Kingdom of God? Be not deceived: neither fornicators, nor idolaters, nor adulterers, nor effeminate, nor abusers of themselves with mankind, Nor thieves, nor covetous, nor drunkards, nor revilers, nor extortioners, shall inherit the Kingdom of God."* We're also told in Galatians 5:19-21, *"Now the works of the flesh are manifest, which are these; Adultery, fornication, uncleanness, lasciviousness,*

---

[26]The Amplified Bible © 1965, Zondervan Publishing House

Principles of Kingdom Living

Idolatry, witchcraft, hatred, variance, emulations, wrath, strife, seditions, heresies, Envyings, murderers, drunkenness, reveling, and such like: of the which I tell you before, as I have also told you in time past, that they which do such things shall not inherit the Kingdom of God."

The Word of God declares that none of those people shall inherit the Kingdom of God, unless they repent. So if we're going to Get Our Relationships Right, we've got to do it just the way God intended. Nobody is perfect, and mistakes will be made, but they can also be forgiven. When David committed adultery with Bathsheba, and Nathan the prophet told him about himself, David began to pray a Song found in Psalm 51 which reads:

> *"Have mercy upon me, O God, according to thy lovingkindness: according unto the mulititude of thy tender mercies blot out my transgressions. Wash me thoroughly from mine iniquity, and cleanse me from my sin. For I acknowledge my transgressions: and my sin is ever with me. Against thee, thee only have I sinned, and done this evil in thy sight: thou that mightiest be justified when thou speakest, and be clear when thou judgest. Behold, I was shapen in iniquity; and in sin did my mother conceive me. Behold, thou desirest truth in the inward parts and in the hidden part thou shalt make me to know wisdom. Purge me with hyssop, and I shall be clean: wash me, and I shall be whiter than snow. Make me to hear joy and gladness; that the bones which thou hast broken may rejoice. Hide thy face from my sins, and blot out all mine iniquities. Create in me a clean heart, O God; and renew a right spirit within me."*

David asked for forgiveness and God granted it. He did so in the fact that the savior of the world still came through the bloodline of David, and I'm talking about Jesus!!!

If we're going to get our Relationships Right, we've got to start with that Relationship – the one with Jesus!!!

Principles of
KINGDOM LIVING
How to Live Right in a World Gone Wrong

CHAPTER
10

SAY WHAT YOU MEAN, AND MEAN WHAT YOU SAY!

"Again, ye have heard that it hath been said by them of old time, Thou shalt not forswear thyself, but shalt perform unto the Lord thine oaths: But I say unto you, Swear not at all; neither by heaven; for it is God's throne: Nor by the earth; for it is his footstool: neither by Jerusalem; for it is the city of the great King. Neither shalt thou swear by thy head, because thou canst not make one hair white or black. But let your communication be, Yea, yea; Nay, nay: for whatsoever is more than these cometh of evil."

Matthew 5:33-37

We spend so much time trying to be "PC" or "Politically Correct" that people are not hearing and understanding what we're really trying to say to one another. Personally, I try to select my words carefully because what I say can and will be used in various conversations and situations. For example, as I share the Word of God through sermons, people hear them, and even find themselves in situations where they say, "Well, the pastor said..." and that becomes the basis for supporting their point of view. I'm thankful to God that He's given me a heart and desire to share and tell the people of God the Truth, so when I'm repeated, God is actually repeated and that's the real blessing!

I've also discovered that in most cases, people can put it out there, but have a very hard time receiving it. What am I trying to say? People are quick to speak their minds, tell you how they feel about things, and even say things in such a way that they hurt others feelings, but when the tables are reversed, they can't handle it! We should be able to talk and communicate with each other in a manner that is both loving and understandable. I believe the "golden rule" is in full effect here which simply says, "do unto others, as you would have them do unto you!" Sometimes, the truth hurts, but it also has the power to set us free! Then it becomes a matter in how we present that truth to one another. So when we're talking to one another– *Say What You Mean, and Mean What You Say!*

Throughout His "Sermon on the Mount," our Lord has been re-visiting Biblical Truths and explaining them for better understanding and application. The Rabbis, Scribes and Pharisees have reinterpreted and in some cases, misinterpreted the Scriptures to the point that Jesus takes the time to clarify what "thus saith the Lord." One thing I've found out about the Word of God is that it is timeless; it transcends all time; outlasts things that are around for a specific time; and has the power to enable us to know the way to spend time and eternity with the Lord! Let's examine the text...

When you Say What You Mean, and Mean What You Say...

Don't Put Yourself Out There Falsely (verse 33)

Here in the text, the Lord has moved from dealing with our relationships to how we should communicate with each other. Here, His emphasis is on making vows, making and keeping our promises, and keeping our word with one another. He uses the word, "forswear" which is from a Greek word that means "to commit perjury," or in other words, don't lie! It also carries with it the idea that we should not make vows or promises we don't have the power or authority to keep.

Dr. Finis Dake shares, *"Making vows by heaven, earth, or any other thing that we have not power to change is forbidden."*[27] This is significant because the Bible teaches us in Ecclesiastes 5:4-5, *"When thou vowest a vow unto God, defer not to pay it; for he hath no pleasure in fools: pay that which thou hast vowed. 5 Better is it that thou shouldest vow and not pay."* This is why we must be very careful trying to make deals with God so He can get us out of our own "self-inflicted" situations. You know what I'm talking about,*"Lord, if you deliver me from this situation, I'll go to church every Sunday morning!"* or *"Lord, if you get me out of this circumstance, I'll read my Bible everyday and even start attending Bible study on Wednesday nights!"* We make these vows when all hell is breaking loose, yet when He brings us through, do we always follow through? So when we deal with God and one another, **Say What You Mean, and Mean What You Say!**

Don't Use God's Name in Vain (verses 34-36)

Jesus now takes and restricts the law as it's been presented by the religious leaders. It was their interpretation that it was acceptable to swear under the right conditions, when it benefited them and their cause. Jesus is now saying that it's not acceptable to swear at all under any circumstances.

For clarification purposes, *The Preacher's Outline and Sermon Bible* shares with us that there are at least six types of swearing:

- "<u>There is swearing by oaths.</u> *What then does Christ mean by saying, "Swear not at all"? Simply that a man's word should be trustworthy in his day to day speech, so trustworthy that no oath is ever necessary. His character should be his guarantee, the only guarantee he needs.*
- <u>There is habitual, frivolous swearing.</u> *The unrighteous are said to have "mouths full of cursing and bitterness."*

[27] Dake's Annotated Reference Bible, Dake Bible Sales, Inc.

- *There is hypocritical swearing. There are some who "bless God" in one breath and turn around and "curse men" in the next breath. James 3:10 says, "Out of the same mouth proceedeth blessings and cursings. My brethren, these things ought not so to be."*

- *There is silent, universal swearing. Every man is charged with secretly cursing others within their hearts. Ecclesiastes 7:22 says, "For oftentimes also thine own heart knoweth that thou thyself likewise hast cursed others."*

- *There is evasive swearing. Some do not use words that are foul, dirty, ugly, harsh, or binding. They would never use God's name in vain. Rather, they choose substitute words – words that are commonly used in everyday conversation, words that would never be considered swearing. Others choose what are thought to be milder curse words. By evading harsh swearing, they feel their word is not so binding. They count themselves less guilty.*

- *There is ego swearing. Many swear to boost their ego, their manliness around others. They feel an identity with the crowd by crossing over to the forbidden."* [28]

Because of the types of swearing that takes place there are times when we have been putting ourselves out there falsely and now we need to convince somebody that we are telling the truth. Then we'll say things like "I swear to God!" or "On my mother's grave! (earth)," or "my hand to God! (heaven)" all in an effort to prove our point. We're told in James 5:12, *"But above all things, my brethren, swear not, neither by heaven, neither by the earth, neither by any other oath: but let your yea be yea; and your nay be nay; lest ye fall into condemnation."* On the other hand, Jesus is saying that if we tell the truth all the time, we don't have to take additional steps to prove our point! It's no coincidence that He's dealing with this issue because it's one of those commandments that God gave in Exodus 20:7 which reads, *"Thou shalt not take the name of the Lord thy God in vain; for the Lord will not hold him guiltless that taketh his name in vain."* We don't like people using our names wrongly or inappropriately, and neither does God! He's going to deal with them in His own way…

---

[28] Preacher's Outline and Sermon Bible, Matthew 1, Deeper Study #1, page 89

Say What You Mean, And Mean What You Say!

Tell The Truth, and Shame the Devil! (verse 37)

Now the Lord drives the point home by telling us to be mindful of our communication. When He was referring to our communication, He was talking about the very words we use and that those words should be backed up by our actions, but more importantly our character. I believe all of us know some who are habitual liars and when they begin to speak we can't and don't believe anything that comes out of their mouths. Jesus says this person is emulating their father the devil who is the father of lies! He tells us in John 8:44, _"Ye are of your father the devil, and the lusts of your father ye will do. He was a murderer from the beginning, and abode not in the truth, because there is no truth in him. When he speaketh a lie, he speaketh of his own: for he is a liar, and the father of lies."_

But you see, when you tell the truth, you are sharing what God loves, and God Loves the Truth! Even Jesus, when He was praying said in John 17:17, _"Sanctify them through thy truth: thy word is truth."_ The Apostle Paul gives us some guidance as to how we should tell the truth and share it with others. I believe it's all about presentation because how you present it will determine how it will be received, and even responded to. In Colossians 4:6 he tells us, _"But let your speech be always with grace, seasoned with salt, that ye may know how ye ought to answer every man."_

If we are going to Say What We Mean, and Mean What We Say, we would do well to follow the example Jesus gave us. Here are some of the things He said and meant:

- In John 6:35, Jesus said, _"I am the bread of life; he that cometh to me shall never hunger."_

- In John 8:12, Jesus said, _"I am the Light of the world: he that followeth me shall not walk in darkness, but shall have the light of life."_

- In John 10:9, Jesus said, _"I am the door: by me if any man enter in, he shall be saved, and shall go in and out, and find pasture."_

- In John 10:11, Jesus said, _"I am the good shepherd: the good shepherd giveth his life for the sheep."_

Principles of Kingdom Living

- In John 14:2-3, Jesus said, *"...I go to prepare to a place for you. 3 And if I go to prepare a place for you, I will come again and receive you unto myself, that where I am, there ye may be also."*

- In John 14:6, Jesus said, *"I am the way, the truth, and the life: no man cometh unto the father except by me;"*

- In John 19:30, Jesus said, *"...It is finished:"*

And when He said, *"It is finished,"* He meant it because He died on Calvary's Cross, and a few days later, He got up from the grave with all power in His hands!!!

Principles of
KINGDOM LIVING
How to Live Right in a World Gone Wrong

CHAPTER
11

LET GOD HANDLE YOUR LIGHT WEIGHT!

"Ye have heard that it hath been said, An eye for an eye, and a tooth for a tooth: But I say unto you, That ye resist not evil: but whosoever shall smite thee on thy right cheek, turn to him the other also. And if any man will sue thee at the law, and take away thy coat, let him have thy cloke also. And whosoever shall compel thee to go a mile, go with him twain. Give to him that asketh thee, and from him that would borrow of thee turn not thou away.

Matthew 5:38-42

Most people, having heard or read these Passages of Scripture would have

Principles of Kingdom Living

some problems with them, especially in the days and times we're living in right now. The average person promotes themselves to be strong, self-sufficient, and willing to take whatever steps are necessary to protect themselves and those they love. That's not a bad thing, per se, but it does cause us to take a closer look at ourselves with respect to what Jesus is saying in the Scriptures.

Finding themselves in the situations before us here, some would say, *"A man's gotta do what a man's gotta do!"* or maybe even, *"I don't have to take that from nobody!"* or maybe if they follow through with the text may say something like, *"After that second cheek, you belong to me!"* Obviously, this is not what the Lord intended which causes us to re-examine the way we do things in contrast to how the Lord is requiring us to conduct ourselves.

There will be people who will come at you the wrong way but that does not automatically require us to go back at them the same way. It's been said that "somebody has to be the bigger person" and that's exactly what Jesus is telling us in this text. Those folks that come at us the wrong way are considered "light weights" as they don't need to be handled by us, but rather by the Lord. So when that happens, **"Let God Handle Your Light Weight!"**

In this text, our Lord is reviewing and revisiting the law that was given in various books of the Law of Moses. *The Preacher's Outline and Sermon Bible* says, *"This law has been used and misused, excused and abused down through the centuries. Man has often used the law to treat others as he wished. But Christ changed the law. He says that the Christian is not to render evil for evil; he is not to bear a grudge or seek revenge. He must go beyond and forgive. However, the Christian has the right to avoid and resist evil for security's sake."*[29] You see, we're quick to retaliate and get back at somebody for what we believe they've done to us, but Christ is telling and teaching us that we as Christians, don't have to conduct ourselves as the world does, but live up to a higher standard and calling as born again believers!

If we're going to Let God Handle Our Lightweight:

---

[29] Ibid, page 92

Let God Handle Your Lightweight!

Don't Give In To Evil (verses 38-39)

Jesus was referring to Exodus 21:24 which reads, *"Eye for eye; tooth for tooth; hand for hand; foot for foot"* and Leviticus 24:20 which says, *"Breach for breach, eye for eye, tooth for tooth: as he that caused a blemish in a man, so shall it be done to him again."* People tend to use these Verses to justify their actions and get back at somebody for a wrong done to them. I find it interesting that they will quote Verses like this but will leave alone others like *"love thy neighbor as thyself,"* but will quickly go to the ones that they believe defends their stance or cause. The Lord wants us to understand that even though someone has done a wrong to us, the Father knows and has the power to deal with them and their actions. The right thing for us to do is to follow the direction of the Lord, but evil always seems to be present. The Apostle Paul says in Romans 7:21, *"I find then a law, that, when I would do good, evil is present with me."* I need to say this, the devil knows how to push our buttons or better yet, what buttons to push! The way for us to handle this would be to take heed to the Word of God as found in 1 Peter 5:8-9 which says, *"Be sober, be vigilant; because your adversary the devil, as a roaring lion, walketh about, seeking whom he may devour: 9 Whom resist stedfast in the faith, knowing that the same afflictions are accomplished in your brethren that are in the world."*

Don't Seek Revenge (verses 40-41)

The word revenge means, *"to inflict punishment in return for (injury or insult)."* There are times when people do things to us that we feel compelled to do the same back to them, or retaliate for what they've done to us. The Text tells us that if someone wants our coat, that we give them our cloak also. With respect to the original Greek here, coat refers to an undergarment, i.e., undershirt, and cloak is the outer garment, or a coat. Let me ask a question; if you found yourself in the situation presented in the text, would you just turn over your belonging, especially, if you feel like you've been wronged? They've taken you to court and the judge sides with them and makes you give up your belongings. I've seen court proceedings on the news when the verdict was given, a family member jump up after the person who has been handed down the verdict. They didn't like the verdict, so they wanted to take matters into their own hands. We don't have to take matters into our own hands, rather put them in God's hands and watch what God can do with them. The writer in Proverbs 20:22 says, *"Say not thou, I will recompense evil; but will wait on the Lord, and he shall save thee."* And we know what happens to the person that waits on the Lord, right? In Isaiah 40:31 it says, *"But they that wait upon the Lord shall renew their strength; they shall mount up with wings as eagles; they shall run, and not be weary; and they shall walk, and not faint."* You see, God has a way to bring about recompense on people exponentially more than we can. God Himself said through Paul in Romans 12:19, *"Vengeance is mine; I will repay."* That's why you need to **Let God Handle Your Light Weight!!**

Don't Withhold A Blessing From Others (verse 42)

Now, somebody might be thinking right now; *"they just slapped me; they just took my clothes; now I'm supposed to just give my things away?"* I didn't say it–the Lord did! What happens a lot of times is that we let the actions of one or a few dictate to us how we are going to deal with or treat others. Someone once said, *"Fool me once, shame on you; fool me twice, shame on me!"* We take that to mean, I'm not going to let you fool me and bring shame on me and so I'll take it out on somebody else! Again, the *Preacher's Outline and Sermon Bible* says here, *"The great Christian ethic is to give. Christ is pointedly clear: a Christian is to help those who have need, and he is to readily help. Christ allows no excuse. The picture is simple: when someone asks, the Christian gives and does not turn away. However, the Bible does not say to give without discretion."*[30] In other words, giving is something that God Requires of us to do, but when doing so, with discretion and understanding. *We are not to cast our pearls before swine*, but in the same token, not turn away someone with a legitimate need. We know there are people out there who are trying to scam us, but there are others who legitimately need our assistance, and we can't let some people stop us from being a blessing to others. The Apostle Paul tells us in Galatians 6:10, *"As we have therefore opportunity, let us do good unto all men, especially unto them who are of the household of faith."* You see, if we want to keep getting our blessings, we've got to follow God's Word with Respect to that. At the Mesa View Baptist Church, we recite a Litany of Christian Stewardship each Sunday during our time of giving, and part of it is found in Luke 6:38 which says, *"Give, and it shall be given unto you; good measure, pressed*

---

[30] Ibid, page 95

Let God Handle Your Lightweight!

down, and shaken together, and running over shall men give unto your bosom. For with the same measure that ye mete withal it shall be measured to you again." When we **Let God Handle Our Light Weight,** He will continue to bless us like nobody else could!!!

I believe the takeaway here is that we know God can handle whatever light weights we have in our lives. We can follow the example of King David when He said in Psalm 18:3, *"I will call upon the Lord, who is worthy to be praised: so shall I be saved from mine enemies."* When we call on the Lord, He can handle our light weight.

You do know that the devil is also part of our light weight? He's always after us and trying to make life hard on us, but God can handle that light weight as well.

The Creation will never be greater than the Creator, yet the devil thought he would try. He tried to take out Jesus in the wilderness; he tried to take Jesus out with the crowd when they all cried out, *"crucify him; crucify him;"* he tried to take out Jesus while He was on the cross but the Father let the Son handle His lightweight!

- Jesus hung on that cross, and the devil was excited
- Jesus died on that cross, and the devil was excited
- Jesus was buried in a borrowed tomb, and the devil was excited
- But Jesus rose from the dead with all power in His hands, and now the devil is worried!

If Jesus can handle death, the grave, and the devil, He can handle your light weight too!!!

Principles of Kingdom Living

Principles of
KINGDOM LIVING
How to Live Right in a World Gone Wrong

CHAPTER

12

LOVE HELL RIGHT OUT OF THEM!

"Ye have heard that it hath been said, Thou shalt love thy neighbour, and hate thine enemy. But I say unto you, Love your enemies, bless them that curse you, do good to them that hate you, and pray for them which despitefully use you, and persecute you; That ye may be the children of your Father which is in heaven: for he maketh his sun to rise on the evil and on the good, and sendeth rain on the just and on the unjust. For if ye love them which love you, what reward have ye? do not even the publicans the same? And if ye salute your brethren only, what do ye more than others?

Principles of Kingdom Living

do not even the publicans so? Be ye therefore perfect, even as your Father which is in heaven is perfect."

Matthew 5:43-48

Being a Christian and living the Christian life compels us to do some things differently. The sin nature that has been passed down to us since Adam causes us to do things the way we want to, instead of most times, the way the Lord wants us to. It's because of sin we're in the situation we're in and it effects every aspect of our lives.

Love is something we need more of especially in the times we're living in right now! As a society, we tend to lean towards the bad or negative things, the evil things, the dirty things, the things that are contrary to God and His Word. I know a lady who does not like watching the news anymore because it's always bad news! For example, if you've watched TV or seen a movie lately there's more things out there dealing with death and destruction than there are things dealing with Love, Peace, and Harmony. They've got vampires, zombies, sexual predators, alien creatures, and the like; all of which are attempting to capture our attention and destroy whatever and whoever is in their path. That does not sound like love to me but just the opposite. There appears to be an insatiable desire to "steal, kill, and destroy" (I wonder if that sounds familiar?) and I believe that's not what God intended.

Because this is so prevalent in our society today, we've been commissioned and commanded by God to do just the opposite of what the world is doing. He wants to us love one another, and our enemies too! That might be a hard thing for some to do, but it's required by God and He's expecting us to do it – not our way, but His way! And I've said before that there are some people out there who are hard to love, but God wants us to **"Love Hell Right Out of Them!"**

In these last few Verses of Chapter 5, the Lord begins to deal with the issue of love. We know from the Scriptures that God's Love has always been there for us even to the point that when we could not save ourselves. God Himself stepped in, showed His love for us, and did what was necessary. Evidence of this is found in Romans 5:8 which reads, *"But God commended*

Love Hell Right Out Of Them!

his love towards us, in that, while we were yet sinners, Christ died for us." Believe it or not, we were the enemies of God in our fallen state of sin and iniquity, but God's love went and goes beyond to Love Hell Right Out of Us!!!

I guess at this point we need to identify our enemy. The American Heritage Dictionary defines an enemy as *"one who feels hatred toward, intends injury to or opposes the interests of another; a foe."*[31] Unfortunately, there are people in our society and probably in our circle of friends and/or acquaintances who fall into that category. The reality is:

- There are people you know who don't want to see you succeed;
- There are people you know that don't want to see you blessed;
- There are people you know that don't want to see you get to that next level in life!

And even though they feel that way, and try to bring failure and drama to your life, God is requiring us to **Love Hell Right Out of Them!!** Let's see what His word has to say about this.

If we are going to Love Hell Right Out of Them..

Follow The Lord's Instruction (verse 44)

In this verse, the Lord gives us four things we need to do regarding our enemies. First, He says to:

1. <u>Love Them.</u> Noted theologian Matthew Henry said, *"Note, it is the great duty of Christians to love their enemies; we cannot have complacency in one that is openly wicked and profane, not put a confidence in one that we know to be deceitful."* [32] As a Christian, it's our duty to love those who have shown themselves to be our enemies. It's by their actions that we come to that conclusion and begin to operate accordingly. The Bible teaches us in James 5:20, *"Let him know, that he which converteth the sinner from the error of his way shall save a soul from death and shall hide a multitude of sins."* It's because of love that we're able to do this. We're also told in 1 Peter 4:8, *"And above all things have fervent charity among yourselves:*

[31] American Heritage Dictionary, Third Edition
[32] Matthew Henry's Commentary, Matthew to John, Volume 5

Principles of Kingdom Living

for charity shall cover the multitude of sins." We're commanded to love them!

2. <u>Bless Them.</u> How do you bless somebody who is working against you? Well, the first thing you can do is not do to them what they are doing to you. We sometimes have the tendency to "get back" at people because of what they're doing to us, but again, retaliation is not our business, that's God's business! The context of this Verse refers to how we speak or respond to our enemies. *The Preacher's Outline and Sermon Bible* says here, *"To bless means that a person has to speak. Christ is saying to speak softly to the curser. Use kind, friendly words. When face to face, be courteous: when behind his back, commend his strengths. Do not render 'railing for railing,' that is, do not condemn or attack him in bitter or abusive language."*[33] If we truly accept the Bible as our final authority, then that's where we need to get our answers. Proverbs 15:1 says, *"A soft answer turneth away wrath: but grievous words stir up anger."*

3. <u>Do Good To Them.</u> Too many times, when we are hurt or offended, we tend to do the same to them who have hurt us. Even though they are hurting us, we still have a command and requirement from God to do the right thing! I know some of you are probably saying, "Ain't no way pastor!" or "I ain't the one!" but it's not my command to you; it's God's command to all of us!! Doing good to them goes beyond words, but deals with our actions towards them. It means to do your Christian duty in spite of what they are doing to you. Proverbs 25:21-22 says, *"If thine enemy be hungry give him bread to eat; and if he be thirsty, give him water to drink: for thou shalt heap coals of fire upon his head, and the Lord shall reward thee."* You see, when you're doing right in the sight of God, it causes your enemies to re-think their approach and eventually leave you alone. The text says that when we do what's required, *"...the Lord shall reward thee."*

4. <u>Pray For Them.</u> It's been said that if you want to see things change around you–start Praying!!!! We say all the time that "Prayer changes things" and I've found out that Prayer changes people

---

[33]Preacher's Outline and Sermon Bible, Matthew 1, page 96

too! When you start praying, there are at least three things you should include in your prayer: (1) Pray that God will forgive them for coming after you; (2) Pray for peace between you and that person; and (3) Pray for their salvation and/or correction. These are things that are not too hard for God and He can handle them if we would just start praying!!! We can take on the Jesus example and principle when He prayed in Luke 23:34 when He said, *"Father, forgive them, for they know not what they do."* It's been said that when you start praying for and about your enemies, it will keep you from becoming bitter, hostile, or reactionary with your enemies!

Be an Example For Your Enemies (verse 45)

Your actions will be reflective of your relationship to the Lord and that might just be enough to turn your enemies around. The text says, *"that ye may be the children of your Father which is in heaven:"* and most children are a reflection of their parents. In this case, we want to be obedient to the Lord and do what He's directing us to do. In doing so, we will reap the rewards and benefits of our obedience. *The Preacher's Outline and Sermon Bible* says, *"Love makes a person like God. God loves His enemies. He causes the sun to shine and the rain to fall on His enemies as well as on those who love him. The Christian is to be just like God: he is to love his enemies. In loving his enemies, the Christian becomes more and more like God. He becomes godly."* [34] The idea here is that if they see us loving they may change their ways and begin to do the same. We've prayed for them already, and now we should be an example for them. 1 Peter 1:15-16 says, *"But as he which hath called you is holy, so be ye holy in all manner of conversation; because it is written, Be ye holy, for I am holy."*

Strive for Perfection (verse 48)

Because of sin, we will never be perfect. But the idea here is that we strive for perfection in purpose. Our purpose should be to do what the Lord requires of us when dealing with our enemies and we should strive to treat and handle all of them appropriately. When we accept Christ as Lord and savior and take on the title, Christian, it becomes our responsibility to live up to that title, and that is to be Christ-like! We strive for perfection because of what Paul teaches

---

[34] Preacher's Outline and Sermon Bible, Matthew 1, page 96

us in Ephesians 4:13 when he said, *"Till we all come in the unity of the faith, and of the knowledge of the Son of God, unto a perfect man, unto the measure of the stature of the fullness of Christ."* We can't get right on our own, but when we get right with Christ, We Get Right!!

Love is not something we should take lightly because in the midst of love, there is power. The Bible teaches us in James 4:7-8, *"Beloved, let us love one another: for love is of God; and every one that loveth is born of God, and knoweth God. 8 He that loveth not knoweth not God; for God is love."* You see, we're required to Love Hell Right Out of Them!

The reason we have to do it is because God did it for us! Continuing on in James 4:9-10 it says, *"In this was manifested the love of God toward us, because that God sent his only begotten Son into the world, that we might live through him. 10 Herein is love, not that we loved God, but that he loved us, and sent his Son to be the propitiation for our sins."*

We were the enemy of God, but God Loved Hell Right Out of Us by sending Jesus to die for our sins. The Bible says in Hebrews 9:22, *"And almost all things are by the law purged with blood; and without the shedding of blood is no remission."* In our case, the blood of goats, bullocks, and pigeons couldn't do it for us, but it took, precious blood, holy blood, untainted blood, the blood of Jesus to take care of our sin situation. My Bible tells me that when they put my Jesus on the cross, they pierced Him in the side, and blood and water came streaming down. And when He died, for the remission of our sins, He Loved Hell Right Out of Us!! But I'm glad that early, Sunday morning, my Jesus got up out the grave with all power in His hands!!!! That's Love!!!

Principles of
KINGDOM LIVING
How to Live Right in a World Gone Wrong

CHAPTER
13

GIVING THAT PLEASES GOD

"Take heed that ye do not your alms before men, to be seen of them: otherwise ye have no reward of your Father which is in heaven. Therefore when thou doest thine alms, do not sound a trumpet before thee, as the hypocrites do in the synagogues and in the streets, that they may have glory of men. Verily I say unto you, They have their reward. But when thou doest alms, let not thy left hand know what thy right hand doeth: That thine alms may be in secret: and thy Father which seeth in secret himself shall reward thee openly."

Matthew 6:1-4

Principles of Kingdom Living

As Christians, one of the main things we want to do is please God in all we do. We want Him to smile at us with respect to the words we speak, the deeds we do, and how we share His Son with others. I wonder what our report card would look like in certain areas of our lives? I read something one day that addresses the issue of our wanting to be obedient and pleasing unto God. It went like this,

"Dear God,

So far today, I've done all right.

I haven't gossiped, I haven't lost my temper; I haven't been greedy, grumpy, nasty, or self-centered. I'm really happy about that so far, Lord;

But in a few minutes... I'm going to be getting out of bed... And then I'm going to need a lot of help.

Thank you, Lord..."[35]

This person seems to focus on the fact that they've not done anything contrary to God's Word up to that point of the day and felt as though they were pleasing God with their actions. I think it's important for us to know that God is pleased when we do what He's commanded us to do, and blesses us for our actions.

Having said that I must ask a question, If God graded us on our giving, would we receive a satisfactory grade? I believe we are to be pleasing to God in all areas of our lives and not just a select few. So how we give to God and His work is one of those areas.

Throughout the Lord's "Sermon on the Mount," He's covered many different areas that effects life on an everyday basis. Having just finished with love, now He moves over to explain to us how to give in a manner that is pleasing to God.

In looking at our selected text, I think we must know what we're actually talking about here. The word, "alms" in verse 1 comes from the Greek word *"eleemosynen"* which by definition means *"compassion, (as exercised towards the poor), beneficence, or (concretely) a benefaction."*[36] The Lord is dealing with how we handle charitable giving and that we do so God's way.

[35]Anonymous
[36]Strong's Exhaustive Concordance of the Bible, Updated Edition

Giving That Pleases God

When Jesus was here on earth, religious people were extremely charitable in their giving. The Pharisees for example, gave 10 percent to God as evidenced in Luke 18:11-12 which says, *"The Pharisee stood and prayed thus with himself, God, I thank thee, that I am not as other men are, extortioners, unjust, adulterers, or even as this publican. 12 I fast twice in the week, I give tithes of all that I possess."* A close examination of this text would lend us to understand their giving was not necessarily pleasing to God because their motives were all wrong. If we are going to have the right understanding of this, our giving should be done without being reciprocated, or not expecting anything in return.

<u>Don't Give For Show (verse 2)</u>

Some people like to do things so they can be seen by others. They want other people to know what they do and how they do it. For them, they receive instant gratification for what they do and it's just the opposite of what the Lord is instructing us here. Here Jesus is telling us not to make a big deal of it by sounding a trumpet, or making an announcement of what it is we're doing. In doing so, we're giving off the impression that we're such good people for helping others and want others to know what we're doing! Jesus said…*"they have their reward."* The Preacher's Outline and Sermon Bible says here, *"There is a wrong motive for doing good. Christ takes for granted that the believer gives and does good. What Christ strikes at is the motive of the human heart for giving and doing good. 1. Giving for recognition is the wrong motive for giving. Recognition is said be to sought by blowing one's own horn in two places: (1) in the synagogue before religious people, and (2) in the streets before the public."*[37] Concerning the Pharisees, Jesus said in Matthew 23:5, *"But all their works they do for to be seen of men…"* I think I need to be clear about something here. It's not always wrong to give WHEN men or people see us, because sometimes that can't be helped, but it is wrong to give SO that men can see us! Jesus also said in Matthew 23:12, *"And whosoever shall exalt himself shall be abased; and he that shall humble himself shall be exalted."* So Don't Give For Show!

<u>Give for God's Glory (verses 3-4)</u>

The person that gives for God's glory recognizes that he or she is not the one doing it, but it's God that's doing it through them. When we are giving and doing things for God's glory, we don't even think about it…we just do

---

[37]Preacher's Outline and Sermon Bible, Matthew 1, page 101

Principles of Kingdom Living

it! What's interesting is what the text says here and that is, *"...let not thy left hand know what thy right hand doeth."* The idea here is to do it unconsciously, because it is pleasing to God. Again, let us be mindful that we're talking about almsgiving, which is really charitable giving, but for the sake of discussion and understanding, we wouldn't normally make an announcement during worship as to how much we're giving? To be brutally honest, some of us would be ashamed to tell the rest of the congregation how much we're giving (or not giving) to the Lord's work!! But then the Lord moves on and tells us to give in secret. You see, we don't have to advertise to the world what we're doing, but when we do give, let make sure we do so for God's Glory! God is so awesome that what we do in secret, He can bless us openly. He tells us in Jeremiah 17:11, *"I the Lord search the heart, I try the reins, even to give every man according to his ways, and according to the fruit of his doings."* You see, if we give our alms with the right motives, God will bless us accordingly–but if we do it so that men can see us–we've already received our reward!!

We make the statement all the time that *"You can't beat God giving; no matter how you try,"* but God has been giving to us since the beginning of time! If there's anybody who knows about giving, it's God. Here's what I'm getting at…

He gave us life…

He gave us a family…

He gave us a place to live…

He gave us food to eat…

He gave us opportunities to succeed..

He gave us knowledge that we Needed a Savior…

He gave us a means to obtain Salvation….

He gave us His Son who hung, bled, and died for our sins…

He gave us eternal life through Jesus Christ our Lord because God gave!

Principles of
KINGDOM LIVING
How to Live Right in a World Gone Wrong

CHAPTER

14

PRAYER IS NOT AN OPTION... IT'S A NECESSITY!

"And when thou prayest, thou shalt not be as the hypocrites are: for they love to pray standing in the synagogues and in the corners of the streets, that they may be seen of men. Verily I say unto you, They have their reward. But thou, when thou prayest, enter into thy closet, and when thou hast shut thy door, pray to thy Father which is in secret; and thy Father which seeth in secret shall reward thee openly. But when ye pray, use not vain repetitions, as the heathen do: for they think that they shall be heard for their much speaking. Be not ye

Principles of Kingdom Living

therefore like unto them: for your Father knoweth what things ye have need of, before ye ask him."

Matthew 6:5-8

In today's society, we're finding new ways all the time to stay connected with each other; we've got the telephone, both land lines and cell phones; we've got Instant Messaging® and Text Messages; we've got email; we've got FaceBook®; we've got Skype®; we've got Tango®; we've got KiK®; and all of these go through upgrades and updates to make them better. God, on the other hand, instituted a program that does not need updating, it does not need an internet connection,nor do we need a cell tower to get connected with God. All we need is a desire to communicate with God and faith to believe that whatever we ask of Him, He is able to provide it!

Prayer is our communication with God in a manner that He has directed us to make contact with Him. Someone once said, *"For the Christian, praying should be like breathing. Just as breathing is the response of physical life to the presence of air, so prayer should be the response of spiritual life to the presence of God."*[38]

In the book, *"The Complete Works of E. M. Bounds on Prayer,"* Bounds says, *"The more praying there is in the world the better the world will be, the mightier the forces against evil everywhere. Prayer, in one phrase of its operation, is a disinfectant and a preventive. It purifies the air; it destroys the contagion of evil. Prayer is no fitful, shortlived thing. It is a no voice crying unheard and unheeded in the silence. It is a voice which goes into God's ear, and it lives as long as God's ear is open to holy pleas, as long as God's heart is alive to holy things."*[39]

We say all the time that there's, "power in prayer," yet it's one of the things we do the least. For the most part, we're quick to ask someone else to pray for us instead of asking them to agree with us in prayer. Let me ask a question with the hope of helping us with our prayer life, why it is we have such a hard time praying? Is it:

- Because we haven't done it in a while?

- Because we've distanced ourselves from God?

[38] Anonymous
[39] E. M. Bounds, The Complete Works of E. M. Bounds on Prayer

Prayer Is Not An Option…It's A Necessity!

- Because we don't believe or doubt God's ability? Or is it,
- Because we don't know how to pray?

If you have accepted Jesus Christ as Lord and Savior, you have every right and a responsibility to communicate with Him to *"let your requests be made known unto Him."* You can get a prayer through because of who saved you!!! **Prayer is not an option…it's a necessity!!**

Here in our selected text, Jesus begins to deal with an issue that is needed, necessary, and required in the life of the believer and the body of Christ. Our prayers to God can bring about change and redirection in ways that no other earthly program can bring about. Having just dealt with how we should provide charitable giving, He now turns to an area of our lives that we all need and should do on a daily basis. Let me throw something out to us and hopefully put some things in perspective:

- If you want to buy a home, you complete an application and ask for a mortgage loan
- If you want to buy a car, you complete an application and ask for a car loan
- If you want a credit card, you complete an application and ask for the credit card

We work real hard making sure our credit scores are as high as possible so when we submit our applications we believe we've done everything necessary to receive what we've asked for. The same principle should be applied to prayer! We should work real hard making sure our "Spiritual Score" is as high as possible so when we submit our prayers to God, we can know without a shadow of a doubt that He's able to fulfill our requests! What do I mean about our "Spiritual Score?" I'm glad you asked, I'm talking about Our Faith! Faith is not natural, it's Spiritual and the more Faith we have, the more we can see God do some amazing things in all of our lives, and the lives of those around us. Prayer Is Not An Option-It's A Necessity!

So, let's take a few minutes and look at prayer.

Prayer Is Not About Being Seen By Men (verse 5)

The second word in this verse is "when" which denotes that it's something that must be done. Notice He didn't say if, but when. Then He begins to deal with those who have the wrong motives in prayer and they are the hypocrites. Some people say they don't attend worship because there are so many hypocrites there, but if your motives are right, you don't have to be concerned about what other people are saying. We have the tendency to do things based on other people's approval and really the only one we need to be concerned about is God! There's at least five things I'd like to point out here:

1. Some people love to pray in public; not being sincere, but to be seen

2. Some people love to pray only in public; it's about recognition not about submitting their requests

3. Some people pray both in public and private; they pray in private, but prefer to pray in public

4. Some people pray much to show just how "religious" they are. They've got a lot to say, but ain't saying a lot

5. Some people pray only while standing. Although standing while praying is acceptable, but to only pray while standing can denote pride, arrogance, and self-confidence. Kneeling shows humility and dependence on God Almighty

Because their motives are all messed up, hypocrites pray to be seen and God wants us to be sincere in our praying. Isaiah 5:21 says, *"Woe unto them that are wise in their own eyes, and prudent in their own sight."*

Prayer Is About Spending Time With God (verse 6)

One of the things I've discovered is that if you are going to do something for God, *His Kingdom,* or if you need God to do something for you that nobody else can do, it begins with prayer! That prayer, according to this text requires us to go into our secret closet. It's a place of privacy so you can spend quality time with God. The devil is quick to try and distract you, but when you get in your secret closet he can't do everything he desires to

Prayer Is Not An Option…It's A Necessity!

do! *The Preacher's Outline and Sermon Bible* says, *"A closet is a necessity. The believer must have a private place deliberately chosen for prayer."*[40] Jesus didn't just have a closet to pray in, but He had a whole mountain! According to Luke 6:12, the text says, *"And it came to pass in those days, that he went out into a mountain to pray, and continued all night in prayer to God."* Your closet is actually a place where you can "still away" and have some alone time with God. Here's three things we might want to consider about our secret closet; it should be a place where we can:

a. Be unobserved to get out of everyone's sight

b. Be undisturbed to get to a place where you can avoid interruptions and distractions

c. Be unheard – quiet to men, but loud and clear to God

And think about this, you want to pray in secret because God is in secret! Isn't that what the text says? You do want to be blessed by God right? If that's the case, then you must follow the directions. This verse says that when we pray in secret that God will bless us openly. I don't know about you, but I want every blessing the Lord has for me! 1 John 5:14-15 says, *"And this is the confidence that we have in him, that, if we ask any thing according to his will, he heareth us: And if we know that he hear us, whatsoever we ask, we know that we have the petitions that we desired of him."* If you want to get your blessing from God, **Prayer Is Not An Option…It's A Necessity!**

Prayer Is Not Vain Repetitions (verses 7-8)

God is not looking for long prayers where we keep repeating ourselves to make it into a long prayer; He's looking for sincerity in our prayers. The phrase vain repetitions comes from a Greek word which means, "to babble much; to use many phrases; to say idle things; to say meaningless things." Just because our prayers sound spiritual does not make them spiritual. Let's be mindful that the devil knows the Scriptures, but will quickly use them against us! He did that in Genesis 3 with Eve and in Matthew 4 with Jesus! For us, the Bible says in Ecclesiastes 5:2, *"Be not rash with thy mouth, and let not thine heart be hasty to utter anything before God: for God is in heaven, and thou upon earth: therefore let thy words be few."* Because God is

---

[40]Preacher's Outline and Sermon Bible, Matthew 1, page 107

Principles of Kingdom Living

Omniscient (meaning all knowing), He already knows what we are going to pray about before we start praying. Therefore, there's no need to make it sound religious when God is looking for sincerity.

The child of God must understand the importance of prayer, and more importantly, the necessity of prayer. It's not an option for the believer of Christ.

- If you want to get your deliverance, you've got to pray
- If you want to get your healing, you've got to pray
- If you want to get your provisions, you've got to pray
- If you want to get your breakthrough, you've got to pray
- If you want to get your blessing, you've got to pray

Jesus knew the importance and significance of prayer because before He did anything supernaturally, He prayed!! Here's one example: the Bible says in John 11 that Jesus got word that His Friend was sick unto death. By the time Jesus got to him (which was four days later), the friend died and had been buried. Jesus told them to remove the stone from the tomb so they could see the power of God operating before their very eyes. The Bible teaches us in John 11:41-42, *"Then they took away the stone from the place where the dead was laid. And Jesus lifted up his eyes, and said, Father I thank thee that thou hast heard me. 42 And I knew that thou hearest me always: but because of the people which stand by I said it, that they may believe that thou hast sent me."* After He was done speaking to God, Jesus turned and spoke to the dead man and said, *Lazarus, come forth.* Jesus prayed and a dead man rose and came out of the grave! Prayer is not an option…it's a necessity!!

To show just how powerful prayer is, Jesus prayed from the cross while being crucified. He prayed, *"Father, forgive them for they know not what they do."* That wasn't for Him, that was for us!!

He prayed, *"Father, into thine hands I commend my spirit."* Then He gave up the ghost and died; but early Sunday morning, He got up with all power in His hands!!

Principles of
KINGDOM LIVING
How to Live Right in a World Gone Wrong

CHAPTER
15

PRAYING GOD'S WAY

"After this manner therefore pray ye: Our Father which art in heaven, Hallowed be thy name. Thy kingdom come. Thy will be done in earth, as it is in heaven. Give us this day our daily bread. And forgive us our debts, as we forgive our debtors. And lead us not into temptation, but deliver us from evil: For thine is the kingdom, and the power, and the glory, for ever. Amen."

Matthew 6:9-13

Praying is something so important that Jesus made it a point to get away to pray. He knew the significance of prayer and the power and potential found in prayer. When His disciples approached Him to teach them how to pray, He made sure to give them a model that would cover every aspect of life during their time of prayer. It worked for them then, and it still works for us now!

I have learned and am learning that when God wants to get a point across, He repeats Himself and prayer is no exception. Here's what I'm getting at:

- The word pray is found in 306 verses of the King James Bible
- The word prayed is found in 65 verses of the King James Bible
- The word prayer is found in 107 verses of the King James Bible
- The word praying is found in 20 verses of the King James Bible

In some instances, the word "pray" is used in the form of asking someone to do something, and when you think of what prayer is, it's the same principle. One thing of note here is that all of these verses are not necessarily commands from God, but rather a combination of receiving God's command and their response to it. When the doctor tells you that reducing your salt intake is good for you, your response should be to reduce your salt intake because of the benefits associated with it. God has given us the command and instruction to pray as there are benefits to them, and our response should be to pray in order to see how God honors His word and His promises.

I have said that prayer is communication with God and that requires more than one person to be engaged in the conversation. There is a misconception regarding prayer that it's a monologue but actually, it's a dialogue. Although we usually spend our time in prayer asking God to take care of our problems, our troubles, our situations, and our circumstances, it's also a time in which we can hear from God. Think about it…when you engage in conversation with someone, you talk for a while and then give the other person time to respond back to you…the same principle is applied to prayer. It's during prayer that we should also give God a chance to speak back to us so that we can "be about the Father's business." It's during prayer that we can apply the words to the song…

"Speak to my heart, Holy Spirit
Give me the words that will bring new life

Praying God's Way

Words on the wings of a morning, the dark night will fade away
If You speak to my heart now."

I'm here to tell you that if you start speaking to God, He will speak back to you and prayer is the vehicle in which we can start the conversation. But if you really want to receive the benefits associated with prayer, then we must begin Praying God's Way!

How many times have you attempted to do something only to realize that your way of doing it was not the best way? For the ladies, maybe you decided to try a different perm, or a different color for your hair, or a different make-up and realized that the way you did things in the past was not the way to use the new product. For the guys, how about the time when you had to put something together in the house, and you followed the picture on the box and not the instructions, only to find out that you had screws and pieces left over? The overall problem with these scenarios is that we've tried to do it our way without finding out the way the manufacturer intended.

The same can be said about prayer and how we should do that as well. In this case, God is the "manufacturer" and we need to seek guidance and instructions from Him as to how He wants us to pray.

Having said that, if there's a right way to pray, then there must be a wrong way to pray. I would submit that praying is never telling God what to do, but always asking God to bless you in those specific areas of your life. I can't speak for anybody, but I don't take too kindly with people telling me what they want me to do instead of asking me to do something for them.

When the individual Christian prays, he or she can see the benefits associated with that in their lives. With that in mind, what benefits can be revealed if the church prays? A praying church is a powerful church–accessing the very power of heaven. Therefore, the true power is revealed when the individual member has a consistent prayer life. Or, what about the church member that does not pray? Do we think their lack of prayer will be beneficial for the church overall? Concerning this non-praying church member, C. H. Spurgeon, noted preacher/pastor and theologian of the 19th century says, *"A prayerless church member is a hindrance. He is in the body like a rotting bone or a decayed tooth. Before long, since he does not contribute to the benefit of his brethren, he will become a danger and a sorrow to them. Neglect of private prayer is the locust which devours the strength of the church."*[41] It sounds to me that Spurgeon is saying "amen" to what Christ when He said, *"...when ye pray, say..."* This is why when we have an understanding of the necessity and importance of prayer, it is crucial that we are **Praying God's Way!**

Here in our text, the Lord begins to break down what Dr. Finis Dake calls the "23 Elements of Prayer."[42] Many people call this text "The Lord's Prayer" but actually it's the Model Prayer. What can be referred to as the Lord's Prayer is found in John 17 when the Lord lifted up His eyes towards heaven and began to pray.

Concerning this model prayer, we find it again in Luke 11 when the disciples of Jesus came to Him one day and asked that He teach them to pray. He proceeded to give them a model upon which they (and we) can use so that we are always **Praying God's Way!!**

What I'd like to do is break down what I'm calling the "23 Elements of the Model Prayer" and briefly expound on each element.

Jesus told His disciples, "When ye pray, say:"

1. <u>**Our Father–That's Relationship:**</u> In order for us to pray effectively and appropriately, we've got to have a relationship with the Father. Just like you can't make a withdrawal from a bank or credit union that you are not a member of, you cannot make a spiritual withdrawal from heaven unless you have a relationship with God, through Jesus Christ our Lord. Jesus Himself said in John 14:6, *"I am the way, the truth, and the life: no man cometh unto the father but by me."* Notice Jesus didn't say "Our Mother" or some other title! There are some people out there that are saying that God is gender neutral – this verse in particular refutes that! We need a relationship so we know whom we're praying to!!

2. <u>**Which Art in Heaven–That's Recognition:**</u> Here we recognize the location of the throne room of God and the place in which

---

[41] www.godwithyou.org/charles-spurgeon-quotes/charles-spurgeon-quotes-on-prayer.htm
[42] Dake's Annotated Reference Bible, Dake's Bible Sales, Inc.

He wields His Power. Isaiah 66:1, tells us *"Thus saith the Lord, The heaven is my throne, and the earth is my footstool…"* The Bible also teaches us in Psalm 11:4 which says, *"The Lord is in his holy temple, the Lord's throne is in heaven…"* When we recognize His presence in heaven, we should also acknowledge that His power comes from heaven as well.

3. **_Hallowed Be Thy Name–That's Adoration:_** The word Hallowed is derived from a Greek word that means "sacred (physically pure, morally blameless or religious, ceremonially consecrated) – most holy (one, thing), saint." Here we adore Him and His name to the point that we place Him and it above all other names and things. God's name is so "hallowed" that He commanded us in Exodus 20:7, *"Thou shalt not take the name of the Lord thy God in vain; for the Lord will not hold him guiltless that taketh his name in vain."* Jewish customs and traditions teach us that God's name was so hallowed that they wouldn't speak it. His name was and is so holy that it was not appropriate to have His holy name come from unholy lips.

4. **_Thy Kingdom Come–That's Anticipation:_** We don't know how long we will be here on earth, but we acknowledge that one day, God's kingdom will come and Christ will be the ruler of that kingdom. We find in Matthew 25:34, *"Then shall the King say unto them on his right hand, Come, ye blessed of my Father, inherit the kingdom prepared for you from the foundation of the world."* We're anticipating the kingdom to come.

5. **_Thy Will Be Done–That's Consecration:_** This is the part of the prayer where we consecrate or commit our lives and service to God and accept what He deems appropriate for us. We recognize that we don't know what tomorrow holds, but we commit ourselves to the One who holds all of our tomorrows. It's here where we abandon our will and totally accept God's will for our lives. Psalm 143:10 says, *"Teach me to do thy will; for thou art my God: thy spirit is good; lead me into the land of uprightness."*

6. **_In Earth–That's Universality:_** The idea here is that God's will

is done throughout the entire earth, and not just in the place where we are located. It's easy and very possible for God's will to be done throughout the earth because it (the earth) belongs to Him. We find in Psalm 24:1, *"The earth is the Lord's and the fullness thereof; the world and they that dwell therein."* Psalm 47:7 reminds us, *"For God is the King of all the earth: sing ye praises with understanding."* As the King of the earth, His will can and shall be done here.

7. **As It Is In Heaven–That's Conformity:** Just as we are to conform to the likeness of God in word, deed, and behavior, our prayer is that God's will for the earth conforms to that which is already taking place in heaven.

- In heaven, there is continuous praise and worship
- In heaven, there is no sickness and disease
- In heaven, there is no death, and it has always been God's will that His people prosper and not suffer

Concerning continuous praise, the Bible teaches us that there are four beasts in heaven whose sole purpose was to praise God. We find in Revelation 4:8, in the "c" part it says, *"...and they rest not day and night, saying, Holy, holy, holy, Lord God Almighty, which was, and is, and is to come."*

8. **Give Us–That's Supplication:** The word supplication comes from the root word supplicate which by definition means, *"to make a humble, earnest petition."* Again, we're not in a position to demand anything from God, but we are commanded by God in Philippians 4:6 to *"Be careful for nothing; but in every thing by prayer and supplication with thanksgiving let your requests be made known unto God."* We accept the fact that God is Omniscient which means He's all knowing and we think there's no reason to ask, seek, and knock; but the problem with that is according to James 4:2, *"...ye have not because ye ask not."*

9. **This Day–That's Definiteness:** We say all the time that "He's an on-time God, yes He is" and that's what we must always hold on to. Because God is Omniscient, He knows what we need and

when we need it. Naturally so, you don't take a cake out of the oven before it's fully cooked, and God doesn't send down blessings until it's the appropriate time for us to receive them. To show you just how definite God can be, Jesus made the statement while being betrayed by Judas and Peter cutting off a man's ear in Matthew 26:53, *"Thinkest thou I cannot now pray to my Father, and he shall presently give me more than twelve legions of angels?"* The lesson for us is that God is so awesome and powerful that if we pray and have faith, He can bless us with what we need not just this day, but right now. That's Definiteness!!

10. **_Our Daily Bread-That's Necessity:_** Nobody knows about our needs like God does! He's even promised in His word to take care of all our needs. Sometimes, because of our needs, we tend to worry and be anxious about them, but even in prayer, we should be mindful that God already knows the needs we have. In Matthew 6:31-33 we're told, *"Therefore take no thought, saying, What shall we eat? Or, What shall we drink? Or, Wherewithal shall we be clothed? (For after all these things do the Gentiles seek:) for your heavenly Father knoweth that ye have need of all these things. But seek ye first the Kingdom of God and his righteousness; and all these things shall be added unto you."* Paul added to this in Philippians 4:19 when he said, *"But my God shall supply all your need according to his riches in glory by Christ Jesus."*

11. **_And Forgive Us-That's Penitence:_** This is where we express our feelings of remorse for the sins we've committed against God and His word. One should never think that because they have a relationship with Christ that they have become sinless. It's because of that relationship that we should sin – less. 1 John 1:9, which was written to believers – those who have a relationship with the Father, says, *"If we confess our sins, he is faithful and just to forgive us our sins, and cleanse us from all unrighteousness."* Much like we can tell when someone is not sincere in what they're telling us, especially when they are apologizing to us for a wrong they've done, God also knows if our penitence, our asking for forgiveness, is real and sincere.

Principles of Kingdom Living

12. **<u>Our Debts-That's Obligation:</u>** *The Preacher's Outline and Sermon Bible says here, "In relation to sin, it means a failure to pay one's debts, one's dues; a failure to do one's duty; to keep one's responsibilities."*[43] We're asking God to forgive our debts, those things we owe Him that we've fallen short of giving to Him. We had a debt out there so high that nothing we did could satisfy it, so God sent Jesus, who, according to Matthew 20:28 it tells us, *"Even as the Son of man came not to be ministered unto, but to minister, and to give his life a ransom for many."* His life became the price for our debt!!

13. **<u>As We Forgive-That's Forgiveness:</u>** As hard as it may be sometimes, we have a duty and responsibility to forgive others just as we want God to forgive us. True forgiveness means you let it go and leave it alone, never to bring it up again, just as God does for us. I've said before that I'm glad God does not treat us like we treat one another because when God forgives, He forgets! He's told us this in Isaiah 43:25 which says, *"I, even I, am he that blotteth out thy transgressions for mine own sake, and will not remember thy sins."* That is true forgiveness!!

14. **<u>Our Debtors-That's Love and Mercy:</u>** We serve a God of a second chance and there are people in our lives who need a second chance from us! I don't know about you, but with me, I'm "waaaaaay" beyond a second chance with God, but He keeps on loving me, and for that I'm grateful!! As we forgive our debtors, or those who have offended or hurt us, we restore them back into relationship with us, much like God does for us! When that happens, God extends Love and Mercy towards us so that the judgment we are due is not delivered to us. Ephesians 4:31-32 says, *"Let all bitterness, and wrath, and anger, and clamour, and evil speaking, be put away from you, with all malice: And be ye kind one to another, tenderhearted, forgiving one another, even as God for Christ's sake hath forgiven you."*

15. **<u>And Lead Us-That's Guidance:</u>** If we are going to do anything for God and *His Kingdom*, we need His guidance in order to do so. Our ability does not compare to the power of God and we need

---

[43]Preacher's Outline and Sermon Bible, Matthew 1, Deeper Study #8, page 120

His guidance to fulfill the will of God for our lives. Therefore, we need the Word of God if we're going to make that happen. Psalm 119:133 says, *"Order my steps in thy word: and let not any iniquity have dominion over me."* Let me say this real quickly....please don't ask God for guidance if you don't intend to follow it!

16. **_Not Into Temptation-That's Protection:_** In this part of the prayer, the idea is that we pray for God to keep us from the pull and temptations of life. There are many things that will try to trip us up with respects to evil in the world, and our prayer is that God would open our eyes and keep us from those very same things. The Bible says in 1 Peter 5:8, *"Be sober, be vigilant; because your adversary the devil, as a roaring lion, walketh about, seeking whom he may devour."* God won't tempt us, but the devil will, so we need God's protection from the enemy's attacks.

17. **_But Deliver Us-That's Salvation:_** There's only one way to salvation and it's through the saving power of Jesus Christ. In the model prayer we're asking God to keep us from the works of evil, that we might continue to live a life pleasing in His sight. Because that sin nature is in all of us, we need the saving power of Christ to be foremost in our lives daily. But in context to the prayer, we need God's deliverance from the power of evil that's all around us. King David said it this way in Psalm 18:2, *"The Lord is my rock, and my fortress, and my deliverer; my God, my strength, in whom I will trust; my buckler, and the horn of my salvation, and my high tower."* Praise God that when we fall, He's able to pick us up and send us on our way!

18. **_From Evil-That's Righteousness:_** The Bible teaches us that our righteousness is as but filthy rags, but when Jesus enters into our lives, we take on His righteousness. It's through prayer that we're empowered to deal with evil and cast it far from us. Although evil is all around us in the world, so is the Lord and He's got power over evil! He reminds us in John 16:33b, *"In the world ye shall have tribulation: but be of good cheer; I have overcome the world."*

19. **_For Thine Is The Kingdom-That's Faith:_** By faith, we believe that

Principles of Kingdom Living

the Kingdom is His and His to rule as He sees fit. Just as the earth is His, so is the Kingdom and by faith we believe it to be so. The Bible teaches us in Matthew 21 that Jesus left Bethany on His way back to Jerusalem and was hungry. He came across a fig tree that had no figs on it and cursed it. His disciples saw the tree wither up right before their eyes and were amazed. He then began to teach them on faith and Matthew 21:21 says, *"…Verily I say unto you, If ye have faith, and doubt not, ye shall not only do this which is done to the fig tree, but also if ye shall say unto this mountain, Be thou removed, and be thou cast into the sea; it shall be done."*

20. **<u>And The Power-That's Humility</u>:** If we are true to ourselves, we would admit that we have no power in and of ourselves. Anything and everything we do is because He empowers us to do so. We don't get up in the morning without Him; we don't move without Him; we don't exist without Him. He's made that perfectly clear in John 15:5 in the latter part which says, *"For without me, ye can do nothing."*

21. **<u>And The Glory-That's Reverence</u>:** By definition, reverence means "profound awe and respect" and knowing how awesome our God is, we should have and show that reverence to Him all the time. It must be important if Jesus included it as part of the model prayer, not to remind God, but to remind us as to how awesome our God is. Psalm 104:31 says, *"The glory of the Lord shall endure for ever: the Lord shall rejoice in His works."*

22. **<u>Forever-That's Timelessness:</u>** In prayer, we recognize and acknowledge the God who has no beginning and has no end. We refer to Him as the Alpha and the Omega, the Author and Finisher of our faith. The Bible teaches us in Psalm 90:2, *"Before the mountains were brought forth, or even thou hadst formed the earth and the world, even from everlasting to everlasting, thou art God."*

23. **<u>Amen-That's Affirmation!</u>** The *Preacher's Outline and Sermon Bible* says here, "When spoken by God, 'Amen' means it is and shall be so, unequivocally. When spoken by man it is a petition meaning, 'Let it be.'" We say Amen because we believe it to be true and therefore hold on to the fact that God is able!!!

Praying God's Way

I want to encourage somebody today that when you start Praying God's Way, you can expect to hear God say "Amen!" Faith moves God; prayers done God's way moves God;

- If you want to see God moving in your life–start Praying God's Way
- If you want to see God bring about change in your life–start Praying God's Way
- If you want to see God bring about deliverance in your life–start Praying God's Way
- If you want to see God change some people around you–start Praying God's Way
- If you want to see God change you–start Praying God's Way!
- If you want to see God send the anointing that destroyeth every yoke– start Praying God's Way
- If you want to see God enlarge your territory– start Praying God's Way
- If you want to see God send blessings that will overtake you–start Praying God's Way

Jesus prayed from the cross and said, *"Father into thy hands I commend my spirit"* and then He gave up the ghost. But my Bible says that after He had been buried, on the third day He got up with all power in His hands!

Great things happen when you start Praying God's Way!!!

Principles of Kingdom Living

Principles of
KINGDOM LIVING
How to Live Right in a World Gone Wrong

CHAPTER

16

LET IT GO!!

"For if ye forgive men their trespasses, your heavenly Father will also forgive you: But if ye forgive not men their trespasses, neither will your Father forgive your trespasses."

Matthew 6:14-15

Have you been hurt or offended by someone and it caused you to rethink your position or feelings about that person?

- They may have said the wrong thing to you
- They may have done something wrong to you

- They may have hurt your feelings; or
- They may have even broken your heart

Because of what's happened in the past, it's hard for you to move forward in the future. The hurt has subsided some, but there's still some pain there and it's hard to move on with your life. This is a bad time to have a very good memory because you just can't seem to "shake" what they did, and every time you see them, you're reminded of their previous actions. The biggest problem with this whole scenario in my understanding is unforgiveness!! Because you've not been able to forgive that person, you are still dealing with those feelings, emotions, and even memories of what took place in the past.

From a physical standpoint, unforgiveness is unhealthy! I make that statement because when you're living like that, you are not living life to its fullest potential. Unforgiveness will have you stressing about things; it will have you losing sleep; it will have you not eating properly; and will even cause you to avoid going to certain places for fear that the person might be there when you arrive. Unforgiveness can put you in a box that can be difficult to get out of, if you stay there too long!

I don't know about you, but I do know that I've done some things that God is not pleased with and am so thankful that He not only forgives, but He forgets too! I would be in very bad shape if God avoided me and made it a point not to be in the places I find myself. I think it would benefit all of us if we could be more like God and just ***Let It Go!***

Here in Matthew 6, our Lord is continuing His teachings in the Sermon on the Mount. He just finished teaching His disciples (and all of us) the Model Prayer and to be mindful of the things we should pray about when spending quality time with the Father, and now He's moving on to explain something crucial in the prayer–forgiveness! I found it interesting that of all the things covered in the prayer, that He would immediately single out forgiveness and begin to explain it. I believe the main reason why it needed to be explained is because to some degree it was a new concept to the people. If you recall in the Old Testament, it was "an eye for an eye and a tooth for a tooth," therefore there was no need to forgive anybody. Now

Let It Go!!

Jesus introduces this idea of forgiveness, even to the point of saying that we should turn the other cheek!

I also believe it's important for us to know exactly what the Lord was trying convey at this point. The same Greek word for "forgive" that we find in verse 14, is also found in verse 12 and that word by definition means cry, forgive, forsake, lay aside, leave, let (alone, be, go, have) omit, put (send) away, remit, suffer, yield up. What's implied here is that whatever it is or was, we should forgive, we should lay aside, we should leave it alone, we should let it be, we should let it go, we should put it away, and we should yield it up! Once we start doing those things, then we can begin to see the benefits of forgiveness!! We can start sleeping again. We can start eating properly. We can go places without fear of bumping in to that person we've had problems with in the past! We can start living again if we would just *Let It Go!!*

What Happens When We Forgive Others (verse 14)

A close examination of the text will tell us that God has placed a condition here as it pertains to forgiveness. The condition or stipulation is that if we would make the effort to forgive others, God would in turn forgive us of anything we've done contrary to His word and commands. We have the tendency sometimes to go into our human data banks and retrieve information about what others have done to us, even how many times they've done things to us. Then we conclude that because they've done it over and over again, it becomes difficult for us to forgive them, having made up our minds that they will do something else to us in the future. In Matthew 18:21, Peter posed the question to Jesus by asking, *"...Lord, how oft shall my brother sin against me, and I forgive him? till seven times?"* If you really listen to what Peter is asking, he's also saying that people should forgive HIM up to seven times as well!! The Lord's response is found in verse 22 when He says, *"...I say not unto thee, Until seven times: but, Until seventy times seven."* The principle here is that as often as we forgive others, opens up the door for God to forgive us. I've said before that I'm so glad that God didn't stop forgiving me when I reached 491!!! (7X70+1!)

What Happens When We Don't Forgive Others (verse 15)

Think about this...God is not bound to forgive us when we won't forgive one another! *The Preacher's Outline and Sermon Bible* put it this way, *"There is the warning – refuse to forgive and be unforgiven. The believer who prays for forgiveness and holds feelings against another person is hypocritical. He is asking God to do something he himself is unwilling to do. He is asking God to forgive his trespasses when he himself is unwilling to forgive the trespasses of others. Bad feelings against a person are clear proof that a person is not right with God."*[44] The bottom line here is that if we truly want forgiveness from heaven, we must start forgiving others here on earth. This reminds me of that passage of Scripture that talks about loving God but hating our brothers. In 1 John 4:20 it says, *"If a man say, I love God, and hateth his brother, he is a liar: for he that loveth not his brother whom he hath seen, how can he love God whom he hath not seen?"* The principle here is that if we want to completely experience the love of God, we've got to love one another, and the same applies to forgiveness – if we want to experience the full forgiveness of God, we've got to forgive one another as well!! Now let's please understand that the Mercy and Grace of God is still in full effect as He deems appropriate, but we must also be mindful that God is expecting us to meet His conditions as it relates to forgiveness!

So if we want to totally feel and experience the forgiveness of God, we've got to **Let It Go!**

I don't know about you, but I think about what Jesus did and went through for you and for me!

> - He was lied on
> - He was talked about
> - He was betrayed by a kiss
> - He was apprehended unlawfully
> - He was taken from judgment hall to judgment hall
> - He was beaten to the place whereas He was unrecognizable
> - He had nails driven into His hands
> - He had nails driving into His feet

---

[44]Ibid, page 125

Let It Go!!

- › He was pierced in His side
- › He had a crown of thorns placed on His head

After all was said and done, Jesus, while hanging on the cross had to Let It Go! He looked up towards heaven and said, *"Father forgive them for they know not what they do."*

If you want your blessing–it's time to Let It Go!

If you want peace of mind–it's time to Let It Go!

If you want joy in your heart– it's time to Let It Go!

If you want to be free from the bondage of unforgiveness–it's time to Let It Go!!!

Principles of Kingdom Living

Principles of
KINGDOM LIVING
How to Live Right in a World Gone Wrong

CHAPTER
17

THE SPIRITUAL SIGNIFICANCE OF FASTING

"Moreover when ye fast, be not, as the hypocrites, of a sad countenance: for they disfigure their faces, that they may appear unto men to fast. Verily I say unto you, They have their reward. But thou, when thou fastest, anoint thine head, and wash thy face; That thou appear not unto men to fast, but unto thy Father which is in secret: and thy Father, which seeth in secret, shall reward thee openly."

Matthew 6:16-18

In this fast-paced society that we live in, there's hardly any real drive or desire, generally speaking, to do different or special things for Spiritual

Principles of Kingdom Living

Growth and development, outside of attending worship for a couple of hours once a week. There's a mindset to do just the bare minimum in order to receive the maximum benefit from God. We've made out our schedules to get certain things done, then fit God in and say that we've met the requirement to *"not forsake the assembling of ourselves together"* according to Hebrews 10:25.

As Christians:

- We know and accept that we should attend worship on a regular basis;
- We know and accept that we should read our Bibles daily;
- We know and accept that we should pray without ceasing;
- We know and accept that we should attend Sunday School for our individual Spiritual Growth;
- We know and accept that we should attend Bible study once a week;
- Yet we do just enough to get by and not enough to get ahead!

Doing all those things I just mentioned will help us grow spiritually, but there's another step we could take that could draw us closer to God, and that's by showing Him how serious we are by abstaining from foods for Spiritual Growth. I need to go on record now and say that as it pertains to fasting from a Biblical perspective, it always dealt with food, meaning abstaining from it in order to draw closer to God. In this day of technology and abundance, some people have taken fasting to a whole new level:

Some people fast from watching TV;

Some people fast from listening to music;

Some people fast from shopping;

Some people fast from their favorite hobby; (i.e., golfing; bowling; football;)

Some people fast from socializing with their friends.

And things like that…

The Spiritual Significance Of Fasting

Now, some of you might be thinking that back in Bible days, they didn't have TV, golfing, football, and all those things that we have today, so they couldn't "fast" of those things. I would agree with you on that point, but I will tell you that we can do without all those things if we wanted to, but one thing we can't do without is, food! God has designed us that we cannot live without food and because it's a necessity, when we begin to fast and neglect ourselves of food, we're showing God just how serious we are about growing spiritually.

Let me also go on record to say that fasting is not a "spiritual weight-loss program" and the purpose for doing it is not to lose a few pounds. If that's the purpose, then you've already missed the true purpose behind fasting. Much like the TV Show, in this case, you will be "The Biggest Loser!" (and I say that in love!)

By now, you're probably wondering what fasting is, so let me tell you what the Bible says about it. In the Old Testament, the primary Hebrew word used for fast is *tseum*[45] (pronounce tsoom), it means to cover over (the mouth) and appears a total of 24 times in this context. What's implied here is not allowing any food to enter the mouth or body. In the New Testament, the Greek word used in our text is nesteuo[46] (pronounced nase-tyoo-o), it literally means to abstain from food and appears a total of 17 times in this context. In the Old Testament, the first time a fast was used in this context is found in 2 Samuel 12:21 when King David broke a fast after he found out his child with Bathsheba had died. The last time it was used in this context can be found in Zechariah 8:19 when God was setting forth the conditions of blessing Judah.

Our text today is the first mention of fasting in the New Testament and if you take a close look at it, Jesus did not say "if you fast," but rather *"when you fast."* Obviously, Jesus was not making a suggestion that we should, but made the statement that as Christians, we would! This is something the Lord is requiring us to do because He knows **"The Spiritual Significance of Fasting!!"**

If we are going to do our part in growing closer to God and obtaining blessings from God, fasting is part of the equation. Although this is the first time the word "fast" is used in Matthew, it was not the first time it was

[45]Strong's Exhaustive Concordance of the Bible, Updated Edition
[46]Ibid

practiced. You may recall in Matthew 4, the Bible teaches us that Jesus was led by the Spirit into the wilderness to be tempted of the devil, and while there He fasted 40 days and 40 nights. It is believed that Jesus went without food and possibly water during this 40 day period. Some of us couldn't go 40 hours. Some people fast every day – the period of time between breakfast, lunch, and dinner!

We have evidence that fasting did indeed take place in and during the life of Jesus and as believers, it should be a part of our lives as well.

The Preacher's Outline and Sermon Bible gives us these four (4) times when the believer should fast:

- *"There are times when the believer feels a special pull, an urge, a call within his heart to get alone with God. This is God's Spirit moving within his heart. When this happens, nothing – not food, not responsibility – should keep him from getting all alone with God. He should fast as soon as possible.*
- *There are times when special needs arise. The needs may concern the believer's own life or the life of friends, society, the world, or some ministry or mission. Again, nothing should keep the believer from spending a very special time in God's presence when facing such dire needs.*
- *There are times when the believer needs to humble his soul before God. At such times he learns not only humility, but dependence upon God. (Psalms 35;13).*
- *There are times when the believer needs a very special power from God. The Lord promised such power if the believer prayed and fasted (Matthew 17:21; Mark 9:29)."* [47]

Having said that, I've got two points I want to cover with this Text:

The Wrong Way to Fast (Verse 16)

Throughout the Sermon on the Mount, the Lord has been giving instructions as to how to do certain things. Here He's clarifying for the believer what's required as it relates to fasting. He makes the point that

[47] Preacher's Outline and Sermon Bible, Deeper Study # 1, page 129

when we do it, we should not do it like the hypocrites, who only want to be seen and known to be doing something. That's probably one of the reasons why so many people claim they don't want to go to church because of so many hypocrites that go there. Let me tell you about a hypocrite in our society – it's the person who goes to work, claims he's worked a full day, yet spent his day on FaceBook, tweeting all day, and not put in a solid day's work. Yet, they want to get paid for the entire day! Say Amen somebody! In this verse, Jesus is saying that the hypocrites want to be seen by men to be fasting so they can look so spiritual, so religious, and have people think they are so close to God. He said they looked sad, they changed their appearance, all for showing people that they are fasting. If I can help somebody today, fasting is not between you and people; fasting is between you and God!! I've said before that there are people in our society who attend worship just so they can tell their friends they went to worship to appear to be good people. They have no desire to change their behaviors, yet attend because of what people may think of them. They leave worship the same way they arrived because they have their reward. We've got to be careful of this because the Bible says in Matthew 15:8, *"This people draweth nigh unto me with their mouth, and honoureth me with their lips, but their heart is far from me."*

I would not want to go to worship and not feel God and be changed by the hand and power of God.

- I need God to change my heart
- I need God to change my mind
- I need God to change my thinking
- I need God to change my tongue
- I need God to change my direction
- I need God to change my attitude
- I need God to change my perspective
- I need God to change my purpose
- I need God to change my eternal destination!!!

Fasting helps me to draw closer to God spiritually so He can bring about whatever changes are needed in my life.

The Right Way to Fast (Verses 17-18)

According to the text, Jesus makes the statement that when we fast, not if we fast, that we should do so in a manner that people don't know we're doing it. Again, people go around telling folks they are fasting to give the appearance of being so religious or spiritual. Jesus is telling us that we should not look like we're fasting, but we should look like we're living!! Remember, our fasting is between us and God, not between us and one another. Therefore, we should conduct ourselves while fasting as if we are not fasting, so that we don't look for people's approval in doing so. Therefore our focus should be on growing closer to God.

One thing I've noticed here is that the text does not tell us how often to fast, but that fasting was and is required.

If we want direction from God—we should fast;

If we want answers from God—we should fast;

If we want clarity about something in particular—we should fast;

If we want to draw closer to God—we should fast!

God tells us in Jeremiah 17:10, *"I the Lord search the heart, I try the reins, even to give every man according to his ways, and according to the fruit of his doing."*

You see, God knows just what we're doing, why we're doing it, how we plan to do it, and the purpose behind us doing it.

So in closing, we must understand that although the act of fasting is physical, it's actually spiritual because of the Who and why we're fasting!

The Lord's dying on the cross was not just physical, it was spiritual!

Principles of
KINGDOM LIVING
How to Live Right in a World Gone Wrong

CHAPTER

18

EARTHLY PLEASURES OR HEAVENLY TREASURES?

"Lay not up for yourselves treasures upon earth, where moth and rust doth corrupt, and where thieves break through and steal: But lay up for yourselves treasures in heaven, where neither moth nor rust doth corrupt, and where thieves do not break through nor steal: For where your treasure is, there will your heart be also."

Matthew 6:19-21

The American Dream basically says that if you work hard enough, do the right things, meet the right people, and stay focused on reaching your goals, then you could have the nice house, several nice cars, two and a half kids (figure that one out!) and not have to worry about how you would take care of yourself and your family. There are other people who will take a different approach to success by heading to the casino and betting all the money they have on trying to hit it big at the craps table, the blackjack table, or the slot machines. Still others will spend great amounts of time and money standing in line waiting to get that lucky lottery ticket for the mega- jackpot and power ball! They've got their formula as to how they pick their numbers: "I use my mom's birthday; how many close friends I have; the number of years at this current job; and break down the year I graduated from high school and college!

There is a mindset in our society that the more you have, the better off you are, but I would take exception to that when I look at shows like *Hoarders*, where you have people with an over abundance of "stuff," but that does not make them any richer or happier. Most times, the "stuff" is trash, old food, or things the people feel they can't live without.

To the hoarder, it brings them pleasure to have all that "stuff" but the problem is that they are dealing with some psychological issues because they don't or can't see that their over abundance of "stuff" is not normal.

Our Lord cautions us that no matter what we have in this world, it's only temporary and if we're not careful, something will destroy it, or someone can/will take it from us. We've got to make a decision at some point if we want **Earthly Pleasures or Heavenly Treasures?**

Continuing His Sermon on the Mount, our Lord now moves His attention from fasting and prayer to what I call, natural or spiritual priorities. We spend a great deal of time all of our lives acquiring things, stuff, possessions, and things that hold sentimental value to us. I'm not saying that it's a bad thing to hold some things close to you, but not to the point that it takes precedence in your life over the things of God! And I think I need to clarify something right here–everything, and I mean everything– we have has been given to us by God, and therefore we should thank Him for everything, and be mindful that none of these things should mean more to us than our relationship with God!

If we understand that as Christians, we are merely "pilgrims passing through," then we should not want to get too attached to anything in this world.

In the text, Jesus here cautions us to be careful what we hold near and dear to our hearts because when it's gone, it may very well break our hearts! Let's look at the text!!

Earthly Treasures Are Only Temporary (verse 19)

Here in the text, Jesus is giving us very good advice about earthly treasures. He starts the verse off with the word "lay" which implies storing things away for a future use. It becomes a serious problem when we hold on to and rely on those things to be there for us in times of trouble. Regarding this passage of Scripture, Dr. Albert Barnes, in his commentary *Barnes Notes on the Gospel of Matthew* writes, *"Treasures, or wealth, among the ancients, consisted of clothes or changes of raiment, as well as in gold, silver, gems, wine, lands, and oil. It meant an abundance of anything that was held to be conducive to the ornament or comfort of life."*[48] It's interesting to me that the more things change, the more they stay the same! The idea or mindset of the ancients sounds a lot like the time we're living in right now. Here's a problem with earthly pleasures–they are corruptible! They're here today and gone tomorrow! If you take a look at the things you have that bring you pleasure (and even necessities fall into that category!), you will find that they are decaying, getting older, or falling apart on a daily basis! The house you have needs a paint job every so many years; you have to update or upgrade the kitchen; the furniture is outdated; the bathroom looks like it hasn't left the '80's; your car needs new tires and an oil change; your clothes are outdated and you "gotta" get the latest name brand items, because you've worn the items so much that they are falling apart! Jesus even warned us that bugs and the elements can and will mess up our stuff. Given enough time, a moth will eat and tear your stuff up, and as good as water is for us, it's not that good for our things! The Bible teaches us in Ecclesiastes 5:10, *"He that loveth silver shall not be satisfied with silver; nor he that loveth abundance with increase: this is also vanity."* It seems that the more we get, it's never enough!! We're also told in 1 Timothy 6:7, *"For we brought nothing into this world, and it is certain we can carry nothing out."* Having that understanding, **Earthly Treasures are Only Temporary!**

---

[48]Dr. Albert Barnes, "Barnes Notes on the Gospel of Matthew"

Principles of Kingdom Living

Heavenly Treasures Are Always Permanent (verse 20)

I stated earlier that earthly treasures are corruptible, but heavenly treasures are incorruptible. There are things here on earth that moth and rust will take out given enough time, but there are heavenly treasures that moth and rust can't touch. I'm talking about things like:

- Forgiveness of sins;
- Understanding the will and purpose of God for your life;
- Godly wisdom;
- Becoming a true child of God;
- Having the peace of mind of knowing that what God has for you cannot be taken by someone else;
- Knowing that eternal life is yours because of the death, burial, and resurrection of Jesus Christ and you've accepted Him as Lord in your life!

What's interesting to me is that Jesus uses the same word for treasures in this verse as He did in verse 19 and in both verses it is defined as wealth! This reminds me of a saying that goes, "One man's trash is another man's treasure!" Here's my point, there are people in our society that all they want is a house, car, money, etc., then there are others who appreciate those things but realize there's something better waiting for them in heaven! You can put a price tag on the house, the car, and know how much money you have, but heavenly treasures are priceless – because they've already been paid for by Jesus!!!

The Apostle Paul thoroughly understood the difference between the two when he said in Philippians 3:8, *"Yea doubtless, and I count all things but loss for the excellency of the knowledge of Christ Jesus my Lord: for whom I suffered the loss of all things, and do count them but dung, that I may win Christ."* And Paul also knew that heavenly treasures are a sure foundation. He said in 1 Timothy 6:19, *"Laying up in store for themselves a good foundation against the time to come, that they may lay hold on eternal life."* Paul knew the difference between **Earthly Pleasures and Heavenly Treasures!**

Earthly Pleasures Or Heavenly Treasures?

It's A Matter of the Heart (verse 21)

The Preacher's Outline and Sermon Bible says here, "A man's heart is precisely where his treasure is. If his treasure is on earth, his heart is on earth. If his treasure is in heaven, his heart is in heaven. The eye illustrates the truth. If a man's eye is good and healthy, then he is able to focus in darkness. A healthy heart is like a healthy eye. It grasps the true treasure, the treasure in heaven. But an unhealthy heart is like an unhealthy eye. It is in darkness, unable to see the treasure in heaven."[49]

I'm glad I understand that God does not look upon us on the outside, but knows what's going on in our hearts. You see, you can have heavenly treasures here on earth if your heart is right with God! Here's what's I'm getting at:

Psalm 4:7 says, *"Thou hast put gladness in my heart, more than in the time that their corn and wine increased."*

Psalm 13:5 says, *"But I have trusted in thy mercy; my heart shall rejoice in thy salvation."*

Psalm 28:7 says, *"The Lord is my strength and my shield; my heart trusted in him, and I am helped: therefore my heart greatly rejoiceth; and with my song will I praise him."*

Psalm 33:21 says, *"For our heart shall rejoice in him, because we have trusted in his holy name."*

Psalm 73:26 says, *"My flesh and my heart faileth; but God is the strength of my heart, and my portion for ever."*

Psalm 86:12 says, *"I will praise thee, O Lord my God, with all my heart: and I will glorify thy name for evermore."*

The only way you can have such gladness in your heart is to have Jesus there!!! When I think about the heart, I think about God's heart and what He did for us. I realized that His treasure is not in heaven, but on earth. His treasure is not the things He created but His highest creation, and that's mankind! His word says in John 3:16, *"For God so loved the world, that*

---

[49]Preacher's Outline and Sermon Bible, Matthew 1, page 133

he gave his only begotten Son, that whosoever believeth on him should not perish, but have eternal life."

When I think about the heart of God, I think about what Paul said in Romans 5:8 which says, *"But God commended his love towards us in that while we were yet sinners, Christ died for us."*

But the one that really blesses my heart is what Jesus Himself said in John 15:13, *"Greater love hath no man than this, that a man lay down his life for his friends."*

And here's what happened:

They hung Him high, and stretched Him wide;

It was on Calvary's cross where my savior died;

They placed Him in the grave and there He stayed all night Friday;

They placed Him in the grave and there He stayed all day Saturday;

They placed Him in the grave and there He stayed all night Saturday;

But early Sunday morning, He got up with all power in His hands!!

He endured the troubles of this earth so that we can have heavenly treasures!!!

Principles of
KINGDOM LIVING
How to Live Right in a World Gone Wrong

CHAPTER

19

WHO ARE YOU GOING TO SERVE?

> *"The light of the body is the eye: if therefore thine eye be single, thy whole body shall be full of light. But if thine eye be evil, thy whole body shall be full of darkness. If therefore the light that is in thee be darkness, how great is that darkness! For no man can serve two masters: for either he will hate the one, and love the other; or else he will hold to the one and despise the other. Ye cannot serve God and mammon."*
>
> Matthew 6:22-24

It is physically impossible for us to be in two places at the same time. Have you ever felt like you would love to be in two places at the same time? Not only is that physically impossible, but I've learned that it's also impossible

Principles of Kingdom Living

for us to give 100% of ourselves to two different masters. There's not enough time, not enough effort, not enough ability, not enough talent, and not enough treasure to go around to more than one master.

Dr. Albert Barnes, in his *Commentary of the Gospel of Matthew* write, *"Christ proceeds to illustrate the necessity of laying up treasures in heaven from a well-known fact, that a servant cannot serve two masters at the same time. His affections and obedience would be divided, and he would fail altogether in his duty to one or the other. One he would love, the other he would hate. To the interests of the others he would neglect. This is a law of human nature."*[50] His comments help us to understand that at some point, we have a decision to make and that decision is–**Who Are You Going to Serve?**

In our text, Jesus is making the argument about double-mindedness. There are people who cannot make up their minds and try to do two things at once. They find that while doing so, they cannot do both of them effectively, and realize that they are not advancing as they could be. The same can be said of trying to serve the Lord and serving the things of this world. Many people have tried to do both, but have found it doesn't work. They hang out in the club house on Saturday night, then make their way to the church house on Sunday morning, only to find out that they're too tired for praise and worship and only go through the motions.

Jesus starts off this text by talking about the eye. He says in verse 22, *"if therefore thine eye is single, thy whole body shall be full of light."* The word "single" here means to be clear or have a single focus. In other words, we can't have one eye on heaven and the other eye on the world because then we can't focus on either of them effectively. He said that once we focus on one, then the whole body will have light. On the other hand, if the eye is evil, meaning wicked, diseased, blind, or full of evil, it causes darkness to enter into the body.

There are two things I'd like to bring to your attention:

We Can't Serve Two Masters

If the devil had his way, he'd have us going back and forth between him

---

[50]Dr. Albert Barnes, "Commentary of the Gospel of Matthew"

Who Are You Going To Serve?

and God, even to the point of trying to confuse us into thinking that his way is better than God's way. Isn't it interesting that as soon as you start to work on your relationship with God, the devil starts to throw things your way to take your focus off God, and back on to him and the world? He'll try to get us to think that the world has so much more to offer us that it's impossible to live without them. He tried it with Jesus in Matthew 4 and it didn't work! Because the Holy Spirit dwells in us, we cannot be enticed by the wealth of this world. We talked about treasures in the previous chapter with respects to homes, cars, possessions, etc., and if we're not careful, those things can become our gods (little "g"). The God of creation is a jealous God and does not want to share us with anything or anybody. He's made that very clear in Exodus 20:3, when He said, *"Thou shalt have no other gods before me."* He's also made it clear to us in Exodus 34:14 which reads, *"For thou shalt worship no other god: for the Lord, whose name is Jealous, is a jealous God."* As nice as some of the things of this world are, We Can't Serve Two Masters!

We Have to Choose Between God and Mammon

In order for us to make an informed decision between the two, we need to know some things about both of them. So the first question I'll ask is, "What is Mammon?" Mammon by definition comes from "mamona" which means riches.[51] This would suggest the things of this world, those things we can acquire, possess, or take as property. There are some people in our society that their home is their god; their car is their god; their clothes are their god; their money is their god; their job is their god; for some people, their spouse is their god; their children are their god. They feel that having those things, possessing those things, owning those things will make them happy. Usually, they don't want anybody riding in their car, want you to shake off your shoes before getting in the car, you can't touch or adjust anything in the car; concerning their house, you have to take off your shoes when you come in; you are only allowed to go in certain parts of the house, and almost everything in the house is off-limits! When it comes to money, don't ask to borrow any, and they spend a great deal of time watching the stock markets to see just how much money they've made in the last few days!!

---

[51] Merrill F. Unger, "The New Unger's Bible Dictionary

Principles of Kingdom Living

God, on the other hand, is not a what but a Who!!! The Bible teaches us that just the mention of His names tells us not only Who He is, but What He is! Let's take a look at the Who and What of God! He's…

Who:	Jehovah-Elohim	What:	The Eternal Creator
	Adonai-Elohim		The Lord our Sovereign
	Jehovah-Jireh		The Lord our Provider
	Jehovah-Nissi		The Lord our Banner
	Jehovah-Ropheka		The Lord our Healer
	Jehovah-Shalom		The Lord our Peace
	Jehovah-Tsidkenu		The Lord our Righteousness
	Jehovah-Mekaddishkem		The Lord our Sanctifier
	Jehovah-Saboath		The Lord of Hosts
	Jehovah-Shammah		The Lord is Present
	Jehovah-Elyon		The Lord Most High
	Jehovah-Rohi		The Lord My Shepherd
	Jehovah-Hoseenu		The Lord our Maker
	Jehovah-Eloheenu		The Lord our God
	Jehovah-Eloheka		The Lord thy God
	Jehovah-Elohay		The Lord my God

My Bible teaches me that my God is the Invisible God. I don't have to see Him to know that He's with me; He's the Immortal God, He's above and greater than our mortality; He's the Eternal God, He has no beginning and no ending; and He's the Infinite God!!!

Who Are You Going To Serve?

I've read that He's Omnipotent, which means He has all power. He's Omnipresent, which means He's everywhere at the same time. He's Omniscient, which means He's all-knowing; He's Self-Existent, which means He's always existed; He's Immutable, which means He does not change; He's Holy, which means He's absolutely pure; and He's Faithful, which means you can trust Him not just some of the time; not just most of the time, but all the time!!!

Having heard the differences between the two, the question before us today is Who Are You Going to Serve? I would submit that the things of this world might make you happy, but they can't give you joy! Who Are You Going to Serve? You might get some pleasure out of the things of this world, but they can't give you satisfaction! Who Are You Going to Serve? You might get a reprieve from some of the trouble of this life, but they can't give you eternal security. Who Are You Going to Serve?

When we couldn't save ourselves, God sent us a Savior who was slain before the foundation of the world. He's the Lamb of God whose name is King of kings and Lord of lords! He's the man who laid down His life for His friends, and His friends are everyone who calls upon the name of the Lord!!!

He was wounded for our transgressions; bruised for our iniquities. The chastisement of our peace was upon Him and with His stripes we are healed. He's Emmanuel, God with us; He's the Rock of Our Salvation and our Shelter in the time of storm. His name is Jesus!!

So the question remains–***Who Are You Going to Serve?***

Principles of Kingdom Living

Principles of
KINGDOM LIVING
How to Live Right in a World Gone Wrong

CHAPTER
20

DON'T WORRY, AND LET THE LORD HANDLE IT!

"Therefore I say unto you, Take no thought for your life, what ye shall eat, or what ye shall drink; nor yet for your body, what ye shall put on. Is not the life more than meat, and the body than raiment? Behold the fowls of the air: for they sow not, neither do they reap, nor gather into barns; yet your heavenly Father feedeth them. Are ye not much better than they? Which of you by taking thought can add one cubit unto his stature? And why take ye thought for raiment? Consider the lilies of the field, how they grow; they toil not, neither do they spin: And yet I say unto you, That even Solomon in all his glory was not arrayed

Principles of Kingdom Living

like one of these. Wherefore, if God so clothe the grass of the field, which to day is, and to morrow is cast into the oven, shall he not much more clothe you, O ye of little faith? Therefore take no thought, saying, What shall we eat? or, What shall we drink? or, Wherewithal shall we be clothed? (For after all these things do the Gentiles seek:) for your heavenly Father knoweth that ye have need of all these things. But seek ye first the Kingdom of God, and his righteousness; and all these things shall be added unto you. Take therefore no thought for the morrow: for the morrow shall take thought for the things of itself. Sufficient unto the day is the evil thereof. "

Matthew 6:25-34

If we are not careful, we will worry ourselves to death over things we really have no control over:

- We worry about our kids;
- We worry about our jobs;
- We worry about our families;
- We worry about our health;
- We worry about this, and,
- We worry about that.

The fact of the matter is that we tend to worry about everything. Have you ever seen someone stress out over the weather? They hear the meteorologist give their prediction, then they start worrying about the weather. They say things like, "Oh Lord, it's gonna storm tomorrow!" or, "Oh Lord, it's going to snow or sleet, or there's a hurricane coming" and truth be told, there's nothing they can do to stop that weather system from coming. First of all, the weather person is "predicting" what they think is going to happen, and they have no control over it; and secondly, no matter how much we worry about the weather, there's nothing we can do to change it. The best thing for us to do is to stop worrying about it and get ready for it.

Don't Worry, And Let The Lord Handle It!

The Bible is very clear that God does not want us to worry about anything and I'll give you a few examples:

- In the Old Testament, we find in Psalm 37:1, when it talks about enemies, it says, *"Fret not thyself because of evildoers, neither be thou envious of the workers of iniquities."*
- In the New Testament, Jesus Himself said in John 14:1, *"Let not your hearts be troubled, if ye believe in God, believe also in me."*

I have found that people who are worriers are more inclined to not have faith in God and His abilities! Worrying is a sign of having little faith in God and if you find yourself worrying about things, then you are not exerting that same kind of energy towards God and letting Him handle things for you. Somebody once said, "If you're going to pray, then don't worry; but if you're going to worry, don't pray!"

Eventually in our Christian walk, we are going to have to get to the point that life for the most part is not in our hands, but in God's hands and then **Don't Worry, And Let The Lord Handle It.**

As we've been making our way through the Sermon on the Mount, Jesus has been dealing with life issues and has given guidance as to how to handle those issues. All of us, every one of us has issues, and when I say issues, I'm referring to it in the plural as we have more than one. Now the Lord is dealing with the fact that as human beings, one of the things we tend to do is worry! As I stated earlier, we worry about anything and everything, and here Jesus is giving us some reasons as to why we shouldn't worry about things. If we can ever come to grips with the fact that God has everything in control, it will take away the necessity for us to worry about anything. Here in the text, Jesus makes some earthly comparisons to help us understand why we shouldn't Worry, and Let the Lord Handle It!

Don't Over Think It! (Verse 25)

The Lord starts out by saying, *"Take no thought.."* I've learned and am still learning that when we spend too much time thinking on some things, we can find that we can even think ourselves right out of our blessings! We'll spend time trying to figure out how things are going to happen, when they will happen, or even if it's possible for those things to happen. By the time we've thought on all those things, we may get to the point of giving up and don't think it's possible any more. The problem stems from the fact that because we can't see how it will all develop, we give up on it – and that's because we've thought about it for far too long. Again, it's no coincidence the Bible teaches us in 2 Corinthians 5:7, *"For we walk by faith and not by sight..."* because, our eyes can fool us and not give us the full picture. I would suggest we take the approach that Jesus mentions in this verse by stating that we shouldn't worry about what we're going to eat, what we're going to drink, or what we're going to put on as far as our dress is concern. Believe it or not, as believers of Jesus Christ, and because we belong to God, that's His responsibility!!! For all the parents, you know that it's your responsibility to feed and clothe the children that God has entrusted in your care, and if you are a child of God, that's His responsibility to do so!! When we know God as Jehovah-Jireh, the Lord our Provider, we can rest in the fact that He has everything necessary to bless us with what we need.

Dr. Luke (the writer of the Gospel of Luke) takes this same verse and expounds on it by saying we should not be doubtful regarding God's ability to provide. I found it interesting that the Apostle Paul says in 2 Thessalonians 2:2, *"That ye be not soon shaken in mind, or be troubled, neither by spirit, nor by word, nor by letter as from us, as that the day of Christ is at hand."* Although the context of this verse deals with the return of the Lord, it develops the principle that we should not be found shaken in mind, or find ourselves doubting the ability and power of God to provide for us!!!

Consider this…if you know that your issues are taken care of, doesn't that give you peace? And when you find yourself with that kind of peace, nothing can shake you! Isaiah 26:3 which says, *"Thou wilt keep him in perfect peace, whose mind is stayed on thee: because he trusted in thee."* We've got to remember–Don't Over Think It!

Don't Forget To Go To God First! (verse 33)

Another thing I've learned is that we also have the tendency to do things backwards! Why is it when we have an issue with somebody that we'll talk to everybody but that person to get that issue resolved? We'll tell other people what's been said, why we didn't like it, how it bothered us, and

Don't Worry, And Let The Lord Handle It!

so on, yet, won't talk to the person that has bothered us. We may go to somebody seeking advice about some things and not consider the fact that God has our best interest in mind always. And if I can say this right here, be very careful who you seek advice from!! There are people out there that don't want to see you succeed, don't want you to get ahead, don't want you to go to that next level, and will give you "bum scoop" only to keep you where they are! If we can ever get to the point of knowing that God knows all, sees all, and has all power in His hands, it would behoove all of us to seek Him first in all things!

Again, consider the fact that God placed in His word the requirement for us to *"seek first His Kingdom and His righteousness!"*[52] That would mean that if we want what God has for us, it becomes our responsibility to go to Him first to get those things. I've said before that we should not make God a priority in our lives, but should place Him in the center of our lives–so that everything revolves around Him. Some people have a problem with that because they try to fit God into their schedules, instead of fitting their schedules around God.

The main reason why we need to seek God is because of His promises. He said that if we would seek Him, we would find Him! I remember playing a game called "hide and go seek" when I was growing up. When I became "it," I had to find the people who went hiding, and a lot of times, I didn't find them because of their hiding places. I'm so glad that's not the case with God because of His awesomeness, He can't hide from us because He's everywhere around us!!

Here's the promise:

- Deuteronomy 4:29 says, *"But if from thence thou shalt seek the Lord thy God, thou shalt find him, if thou seek him with all thy heart, and with all thy soul."*

- Psalm 4:10 says, *"And they that know thy name will put their trust in thee: for thou Lord, hast not forsaken them that seek thee."*

- Amos 5:4 says, *"For thus saith the Lord unto the house of Israel, Seek ye me, and ye shall live:"*

---

[52]Matthew 6:33, paraphrased

Principles of Kingdom Living

When you understand the promise, you can also understand what God meant in verse 33 when He said, *"...and all these things shall be added unto you."* What's implied here is all the things Jesus was talking about earlier in the text, and if you can have enough faith that God can provide those necessities for you, it helps you to understand that God can supply all your needs according to His riches in glory by Christ Jesus!

God does not want us to worry about anything, but to seek Him about everything!!! We know and understand that we don't have control over our lives, so we must seek out the One who has the control!

He's got control over life because He's the giver of life;

He's got control over sickness because He's the great physician;

He's got control over the elements because He walks on water;

He's got control over the wind because He told it to be still;

He's got control over infirmities because He's healed deformities in people's bodies;

He's got control over religion because He's our great High Priest;

He's got control over the devil because He can't be tempted by him;

He's got control over death because He gave His life as a ransom for many;

He's got control over the grave because the grave couldn't hold Him;

He's got control over principalities and powers because He's got all power in His hands!

That's the kind of power that can take away your worry, take away your stress; take away your frustrations; take away your doubt; take away your confusion!

At some point in our lives, we've got to make it up in our minds that we are not going to Worry anymore, and Let the Lord Handle It!!!

Principles of
KINGDOM LIVING
How to Live Right in a World Gone Wrong

CHAPTER

21

CHECK YOURSELF BEFORE YOU WRECK YOURSELF

"Judge not, that ye be not judged. For with what judgment ye judge, ye shall be judged and with what measure ye mete, it shall be measured to you again. And why beholdest thou the mote that is in thy brother's eye, but considerest not the beam that is in thine own eye? Or how wilt thou say to thy brother, Let me pull out the mote out of thine eye; and, behold, a beam is in thine own eye? Thou hypocrite, first cast out the beam out of thine own eye; and then shalt thou see clearly to cast out the mote out of thy brother's eye.

Matthew 7:1-5

Principles of Kingdom Living

We live in a world and within a society whereby it's been ingrained in us that the things that happen to us are never our fault. It appears that somebody is always in our way; somebody is always trying to stop us; somebody is always trying to hinder us; somebody is always trying to keep us from the things we really want to do and accomplish.

Now, I'm not saying that everything bad that happens in your life is because you're a bad person; I'm saying that there are some things that have happened because of some bad decisions that were made, and now we've felt the brunt of those decisions. Please keep in mind that the principle of God is always in effect, and I'm referring to the one found in Galatians 6:7 which reads, *"Be not deceived; God is not mocked: for whatsoever a man soweth, that shall he also reap."*

As we live, bad things happen and we don't take into consideration that maybe, just maybe, it happened because of our own actions and motives. It's easy for us to blame it on somebody else, when actually some of the blame might rest with us. For example:

> Some people can't seem to figure out why they're having a hard time at work because the boss always seems to be on them; yet, they go to work late and want to get off early every day.

> Some people can't seem to figure out why they can't get a job; yet they haven't submitted an application or resume for a job.

> Some people can't seem to figure out why they're having such a hard time financially; yet they haven't submitted to God's financial plan.

> Some people can't seem to figure out why they're having issues with their bodies today; yet they abused their bodies for many years in the past.

> Some people can't seem to figure out why they're catching hell right now; yet they've been raising hell along the way!!!

There are times when we begin to ask questions like, "Why are these things happening to me?" or "Why is this happening to me, right now?" or even make statements like, "When it rains, it pours!" I've had days like that, and I will tell you that a lot of those days and the events that happened were not because I

Check Yourself Before You Wreck Yourself

made bad decisions, but because God was doing something in my life to get me ready for my next assignment. At some point, we must take a good look at ourselves and see what we're doing as it pertains to kingdom building, and see if it is in alignment with God's plans for us. Remember, this life we live is not our own; the Bibles says, *"we've been bought with a price"* and therefore, we have the obligation to live according to God's design and His will for us. Every day we have to take a good look at ourselves and see what we're doing. Why? Because you've got to **Check Yourself, Before You Wreck Yourself!**

Here in the Gospel of Matthew, Jesus is continuing His preaching on the "Sermon on the Mount" and in doing so, He's dealing with the things and issues that apply to everyday life. By way of review, He dealt with the Laws of Moses, restitution and prayer, committing adultery, divorce and re-marriage, making vows, retaliation, and the fact that we are commanded to love our neighbors, our enemies, and to bless those people who curse us. That's a tall order, but it's what the Lord commanded us to do. I've said before that I'm glad the Lord doesn't treat us like we treat each other because as soon as somebody hurts us or does something we don't like, we cut them loose and don't want to have anything to do with them. In some cases, we'll do to them what they've done to us, instead of "holding our peace and let the Lord fight our battles." We'll find ourselves in the same trap they're in and can't figure out why things are not working in our lives. I'm so glad God forgives and forgets!!

At the beginning of chapter 7, the Lord is dealing with how we should look at ourselves before we start looking at other people. I believe that if you want the people around you to change, maybe the change should start with you! We should never get to the point of thinking that we don't have any room for improvement, but that God can make improvements on us whenever He so desires; we just have to be willing to accept those adjustments. Let's take a look at the text.

Don't Be Judgmental (Verses 1-2)

The word "judge" here means to try, condemn, or punish,[53] much like the responsibility of a judge in a legal proceeding. It carries with it the idea of being above or better to some degree thereby having the "right" to look down on other people. *The Preacher's Outline and Sermon Bible* defines it as *"to criticize, condemn, judge, censor. It is fault-finding; it is being picky."*[54] They give six reasons why people tend to judge and criticize:

[53] Strong's Exhaustive Concordance of the Bible
[54] Preacher's Outline and Sermon Bible, Matthew 1, page 144

Principles of Kingdom Living

1. "Criticism boosts our own self-image.
2. Criticism is simply enjoyed.
3. Criticism makes us feel that our own lives (morality and behavior) are better than the person who failed.
4. Criticism helps us justify the decisions we have made and the things we have done throughout our lives.
5. Criticism points out to our friends how strong we are.
6. Criticism is an outlet for hurt and revenge."[55]

None of us have the right to judge or criticize anybody because we've all done something or "some things" that were not pleasing in the sight of God. The Bible teaches us in Romans 3:10, *"As it is written, There is none righteous, no, not one."* It further goes on to state in Romans 3:23, *"For all have sinned, and come short of the glory of God."*

The reason why we shouldn't be judgmental can be found in verse 2 of our text. Jesus said that the very same things we're being judgmental about will come back on us at some point in time. It's kind of like, "if you put it out there, you can expect it come around again." The Bible teaches us in James 3:1-2a, *"My brethren, be not many masters, knowing that we shall receive the greater condemnation. For in many things we offend all..."* I believe the Apostle Paul gave us very good instructions pertaining to being judgmental and that word can be found in Romans 2:1 which reads, *"Therefore thou art inexcusable, O man, whosoever thou art that judgest: for wherein thou judgest another, thou condemnest thyself; for thou that judgest doest the same things."* You see, we can't get away from the fact that we have our own baggage to deal with so it doesn't do anybody any good to constantly find fault with others. As a matter of fact, when someone is having a hard time, that's the time for us to show some compassion to help them, and not hurt them with our words or personal agendas. Don't Be Judgmental.

Don't Look Out, Look In (Verses 3-4)

Here in the text, Jesus identified that people have the tendency to look out at others, but don't see what's going on within themselves. Maybe they don't want to put the mirror up and take a good look at themselves, but feel better at

---

[55]Ibid, page 145

looking out to others. Jesus talks about a mote and a beam. To put it in context, a "mote" is like a small twig or piece of straw and a "beam" is like a branch or a stick of timber. Maybe we can look at it as the "elephant in the room!" We know something's wrong, but won't deal with it in the hopes that it will walk away at some point. The idea here is that we'll identify little things in others but won't take a few minutes to really look at the big things going on within ourselves. In 1 Peter 4:17, the Word of God reads, *"For the time is come that judgment must begin at the house of God: and if it first begin at us, what shall the end be of them that obey not the gospel of God?"* Just as judgment will begin with the house of God, we should begin with ourselves before we start to identify some problem areas with others. Keep in mind that every time you point your finger at somebody, at least three fingers are pointing back at you! I believe the Williams Brothers, a gospel singing group, said it best when they said, "Sweep around your own front door, before you try to sweep around mine."

I like what Jeremiah said in Lamentations 3:40; he said, *"Let us search and try our ways, and turn again to the Lord."* Let's take the steps necessary to make sure we're good with God before we try to run interference on other people. Don't Look Out, Look In.

Don't Be A Hypocrite (verse 5)

Notice what Jesus called people who are judgmental–hypocrites! A hypocrite is "a person who pretends to have virtues, moral or religious beliefs principles, etc., that he or she does not actually possess, especially a person whose actions believe stated beliefs."[56] In other words, what you see is not necessarily what you get!

> They might be playing the game, but they're not in the game;
> They might be going to church, but they're not the actual church;
> They might look holy, but they don't live holy;
> They might talk the talk, but they don't walk the walk;

The Lord is looking for some real folks, some real people who will check themselves before they wreck themselves. The way we avoid being a hypocrite is by following the Word of God. The Bible tells us in Isaiah 1:6, *"Wash you,*

---

[56]Dictionary.com

Principles of Kingdom Living

make you clean, put away the evil of your doings from before mine eyes; cease to do evil." The Apostle Paul reminds us in 2 Corinthians 7:1, *"Having therefore these promises, dearly beloved, let us cleanse ourselves from all filthiness of the flesh and spirit, perfecting holiness in the fear of God."*

You might be asking yourself, what promises has the Lord made to us? Well, I'm glad you asked that question.

- He promised us abundant life in John 10:10;
- He promised to go prepare a place for us in John 14:2;
- He promised to come back to get us in John 14:3;
- He promised that if we abide in Him, we shall ask what we will and it shall be done unto us in John 15:7;
- He promised never to leave us nor forsake us in Hebrews 13:5.

But you can't have these promises unless you get your relationship right with Jesus.

- He's the offspring and root of David;
- He's the Bright and Morning Star;
- He's the Savior of the World;
- He's the Messiah who came down from Heaven;
- He's the King of kings, and the Lord of lords;
- He's the Alpha and the Omega;
- He's the Great I AM!

Now, He gives us the power to walk right; the power to talk right; the power to live right, the power to give right, the power pray right; the power to stay where we need to stay in Him!!

If we don't know Him for ourselves, we will wreck ourselves and spend eternity in the Lake of Fire!

If you don't know Him today, **Check Yourself, Before You Wreck Yourself!!**

Principles of
KINGDOM LIVING
How to Live Right in a World Gone Wrong

CHAPTER

22

THE PRECIOUSNESS OF THE WORD OF GOD

"Give not that which is holy unto the dogs, neither cast ye your pearls before swine, lest they trample them under their feet, and turn again and rend you."

Matthew 7:6

There are some things that are precious to us such as gold, silver, diamonds and other gems. There are some other things that are precious to us like items we've received from loved ones that have sentimental value. Still there are some other things that are precious to us like our friendships and relationships with certain people and because of them, we cherish them and also protect them as well. We'll find ourselves getting upset when someone messes with or disturbs those things and people that are precious to us because they bring us a certain level of joy and satisfaction.

I would submit to you today that the Word of God is one of those precious and sacred things. It is something that we should both cherish and protect, as it has the power to provide us with the knowledge necessary to obtain eternal life, and be assured of the promises contained therein.

I've got a question for you…have you ever tried to give someone advice that you know will work for them, yet they refused to hear you out? No matter how hard you tried to convince them of the advice, they wanted nothing to do with it, so eventually you gave up and turned them over to their own vices. The same can be said about the Word of God. Believe it or not, there are some people out there who do not want to hear what you have to say about the Bible, nor do they want to hear about the central figure in the Bible. Dr. Finis Dake writes, *"The whole Bible centers around the person and work of Jesus Christ. In the Old Testament, we have hundreds of predictions, and in the New Testament, we have the fulfillment and continuation of His life and ministry. He, Himself claimed to have been sent by God. He performed miracles to confirm His mission; what He foretold came to pass and will yet come to pass. He put His seal upon the genuineness and authenticity of the Old Testament."*[57]

Because some people will not receive what we would like to share with them it requires us to discern just how far we should go in order to share with them. When it comes to sharing our faith, we must understand **The Preciousness of the Word of God.**

In this portion of the Sermon on the Mount, Jesus has been dealing with the fact that we should not judge anyone because it could come back on us, and now He moves on to deal with how we should handle sacred things. He starts off the verse by saying, *"Give not"* which is a direct command to us to not give the specified item away. If you think about it, it sounds a lot like the format given us in the Ten Commandments. There it says, *"Thou shalt not"* and here He's saying *"Give not."* I want to take just a few minutes to look at what He's referring to here.

---

[57] Dake's Annotated Reference Bible, Dake's Bible Sales, Inc.

The Preciousness Of The Word Of God

He Calls it Holy

The statement, *"that which is holy"* carries with it the idea of things dedicated and committed to God. Dake says here, *"Do not force truth upon rebels who reject it, or give holy things to fault-finders, mote-hunters, or evil speakers."*[58] There are people in the world who don't want anything to do with truth as we believe and accept it, and will do whatever is necessary to stay clear of you. Jesus then uses the word, "pearl", which is a precious jewel in society. Naturally so, a pearl takes time to develop and some are more expensive than others. God's Word didn't come to us overnight, but He used 40 authors over a period of approximately 1500 years to put together a collection of books, inspired by Him to give us something precious. There's a few passages of Scripture in Psalm 119 and Proverbs 30 that sums it up for us. It's there we find:

- Psalm 119:89, *"For ever, O Lord, thy word is settled in heaven."*
- Psalm 119:140, *"Thy word is very pure: therefore thy servant loveth it."*
- Psalm 119:160, *"The word is true from the beginning: and every one of thy righteous judgment endureth forever."* And,
- Proverbs 30:5, *"Every Word of God is pure: he is a shield unto them that put their trust in him."*

His word is holy, it's like a pearl, and we should handle it as the precious living word that it is!

He Calls Them Dogs and Swine

Let me go on record and say that I believe Jesus was very specific in His choice of words here. Although the Greek words translates as dogs and swine, or pigs, what's implied is the class of people they represent. *The Pulpit Commentary* says here, *"While you are not to be censorious towards brethren, you must recognize the great and fundamental differences that there are between men. You must not treat those who are mere dogs and swine as if they were able to appreciate either the holiness or the beauty and wealth of spiritual truth."*[59]

---

[58]Ibid, Matthew 7:6, note "r"
[59]The Pulpit Commentary, Matthew, Volume VX, Hendrickson Publishers

Concerning those classes of people, what's implied here are those folks who are despised; those under Satanic powers; wicked men; false prophets; fools; in those days, Gentiles, and Backsliders. When you look at these people, you will find that they are already convinced in what they believe and will not normally budge from that belief. We have the mandate to share the gospel with them, but understand that some people will never accept the gospel truth. This mandate is found in Ezekiel 3:18-19 which says, *"When I say unto the wicked, Thou shalt surely die; and thou givest him not warning, nor speakest to warn the wicked from his wicked way, to save his life; the same wicked man shall die in his iniquity; but his blood will I require at thine hand. 19 Yet if thou warn the wicked, and he turn not from his wickedness, nor from his wicked way, he shall die in his iniquity; but thou hast delivered thy soul."* Let's be mindful that not everyone will spend eternity with Jesus, but we can do our part to at least share it, and give them an opportunity to respond.

He Tells What They Will Do

Not everyone will appreciate what you do and what you say to them. Even though sharing the gospel is the best news possible for any time, season, or society, there are many who will outright refuse it. Jesus says those who are exposed to it and don't want it will trample all over it. In some Muslim countries, one of the highest forms of disrespect is to either show someone the bottom of your shoe, or to step on someone. If you think about what the dogs and swine are doing, they are showing their outright disrespect for what they're being given.

Jesus knows a lot about this because when He came to this world, we're told in John 1:11, *"He came unto his own, and his own received him not."* I think about what Jesus did in spite of how they rejected Him and He still died for them!

When I look at the word, I'm mindful of not what the word is, but who the Word is! The Gospel of John shows us the deity of Christ and shows Him to be God.

- In John 1:1 we find, *"In the beginning was the Word, and the Word was with God, and the Word was God."*

The Preciousness Of The Word Of God

- In John 1:3 we find, *"All things were made by him; and without him was not any thing made that was made."*
- In John 1:14 we find, *"And the Word was made flesh and dwelt among us, (and we beheld his glory, the glory of the only begotten of the Father,) full of grace and truth."*

God the Father knew that all of sinful man would not receive His gift of salvation, but made it available anyway because of His love for mankind. The Bible says in John 3:16, *"For God so loved the world, that he gave his only begotten Son, that whosoever believeth on him should not perish, but have everlasting life."* The Father gave the Son, and the Son gave His life. In the Old Testament, blood was shed for the atonement of sin, and in the New Testament, Jesus' blood was shed for the remission of sin. In other words, Jesus died to pay the price for your sins and mine! But how did He die? I'm glad you asked–He died on a cross in a place called Calvary....

Principles of Kingdom Living

Principles of
KINGDOM LIVING
How to Live Right in a World Gone Wrong

CHAPTER

23

THE KEYS TO RECEIVING FROM GOD

"Ask, and it shall be given you; seek, and ye shall find; knock, and it shall be opened unto you: For every one that asketh receiveth; and he that seeketh findeth; and to him that knocketh it shall be opened. Or what man is there of you, whom if his son ask bread, will he give him a stone? Or if he ask a fish, will he give him a serpent? If ye then, being evil, know how to give good gifts unto your children, how much more shall your Father which is in heaven give good things to them that ask him?"

Matthew 7:7-11

Principles of Kingdom Living

One of the greatest resources given to the church, and probably the most under utilized, is prayer! If you were to take a look through the Bible, you will find that people have been praying since the beginning of recorded time, and they have been receiving answers and blessings from God. Prayer must be important as Jesus Himself made it a point to "still away" from His disciples and the crowd, so He would spend time with the Father in His "prayer closet." Let me ask a question–is there room for you in your prayer closet? Have you put things in there that would not allow you the room necessary to get in there and "get a prayer through?" I'm talking about things like, "I don't have time to spend any time in my prayer closet," or "I can do things on my own and don't need a prayer closet." Are there cobwebs in your prayer closet due to lack of use and occupancy? Are there other things occupying your prayer closet space because you haven't been occupying it yourself? God gives us 24 hours in a day and some of that time should be dedicated to spending quality time with God, building our relationship with Him, and sending up our petitions regarding those things in life that only He can do for us!

Another thing I've noticed about prayer is that it's free! It only costs you a little bit of the time God has blessed you with. We tend to devalue things that are free because there's no price or sacrifice associated with it. I'll tell you one thing, if you're alive today, it's because somebody sacrificed a great deal of their time praying for you and yours and we should not take that lightly.

> - I'm glad my momma prayed for me when I wouldn't even pray for myself;
> - I'm glad my pastors prayed for me before I realized my mission and purpose in the church;
> - I'm glad Jesus prayed for me even before I physically entered into the world.

One song said, "Prayer is the key; faith unlocks the door" so if you want to be the recipient of the bountiful blessings of God, you must understand **The Keys To Receiving From God!**

Now that the Lord has dealt with why we should not judge people, and given us clear instructions as to how we should handle His word, He turns His focus on how we can receive from God those things only He has the power to provide. Too many times, we do things just the opposite from what He's told us to do. Here's what I'm talking about—when it comes to getting our needs taken care of, we naturally tend to turn to people to get from them that which only God can give us; or we look to people and when they can't provide, we get disappointed, then eventually turn to God. Matthew 6:33 says, *"But seek ye first the Kingdom of God and his righteousness, and all these things shall be added unto you."* The way we seek God first is to turn to Him in prayer, and according to His word, *"…let our requests be made known unto him."*

Here the Lord gives us three things we need to do in order to receive from God. Here's what He said;

We're Commanded To Ask

The Greek word for ask here is *aiteo* (pronounced ate-tee-o) and carries with it the idea to ask, beg, call for, desire, or crave.[60] When we go before God in prayer, most times it's not to acknowledge or adore Him, it's usually because we want something from Him. Jesus is telling us here that one of the keys to receiving from God is to ask of God! We're quick to say that He's got all power in His hands; we're quick to say, *"The earth is the Lord's and the fullness thereof; the world and they that dwell therein."*[61] We're quick to say, "the silver is His and the gold is His,"[62] yet we won't go to Him first when we need things from Him. For parents, we're quick to tell our children that if they want something, they need to learn how to ask for them and then we will consider giving those things asked to them. We even tell them there's a certain way of asking in order to receive. Check this out—none of us are in a position to demand anything from God, but if we ask in the manner He's instructed us, He's promised to respond. Jesus Himself said in verse 8 of our text, *"For every one that asketh receiveth;"* I don't know about you, but I'm glad that when I find myself in obedience with God, He's got the power to bless me with what I ask of Him, according to His will. We've got to apply **The Keys to Receiving From God!**

We're Commanded to Seek

What does it mean to seek? Seeking means to go looking for something or make the attempt to find what you are looking for. I need to be real right here—too many times in Christiandom, we've made it up in our minds that

---

[60] Strong's Exhaustive Concordance of the Bible, Third Edition
[61] Psalm 24:1, [62] Haggai 2:8, paraphrased

as long as we have faith, whatever we're in need of will come to us, without us having to do anything! My Bible teaches that *"faith without works is dead"* and therefore, we've got to do something with our faith. King David said in Psalm 105:4-5, *"Seek the Lord, and his strength: seek his face evermore. 5 Remember his marvelous works that he hath done; his wonders, and the judgments of his mouth."* When we're commanded to do something, the Lord tells us that we will get results when we operate in obedience. Again, Jesus promises us in verse 8 of our text, *"…and he that seeketh findeth."* Further evidence of this can be found in Deuteronomy 4:29 which reads, *"But if from thence thou shalt seek the LORD thy God, thou shalt find him, if thou seek him with all thy heart and with all thy soul."*

We're Commanded To Knock

To knock would imply that there's something on the other side of the door that you want to have or get to. The key is to take the necessary action to get the door opened so you can get what's on the other side of the door. *The Preacher's Outline and Sermon Bible* says,

"The word 'knock' says the following: (a) We knock when we are shut out and need or want entrance; (b) We knock when there is someone on the other side who can open to us."[63]

In both of those instances, there is something or someone on the other side that requires us to knock so we can have access. Let me ask a question, do you drive to someone's house, park your car in front of the house, and wait for them to come outside to greet you? In most cases, you get out of your car, go up to the door and knock or ring the doorbell. You have something to do in order to get to the person or the thing on the other side of the door!

So we must understand that if we are going to receive from God, we have to do our part to ask, seek, and knock. All three of these words are verbs, which means they are action words! It requires us to do something in order to receive. If you want to get paid, you've got to go to work; if you want to graduate, you've got to go to school; and if you want to receive from God, you've got to ask!

---

[63]Preacher's Outline and Sermon Bible, Matthew 1, Deeper Study #1, page 150

Principles of
KINGDOM LIVING
How to Live Right in a World Gone Wrong

CHAPTER
24

THE GOLDEN RULE

"Therefore all things whatsoever ye would that men should do to you, do ye even so to them: for this is the law and the prophets."

Matthew 7:12

I believe everybody wants to be treated fairly, with respect, and feel appreciated. One of the ways to ensure this happens to you is to do it to other people and it will come back to you. This principle is found in several places in the Bible and says the same thing. In Galatians 6:7, the Apostle Paul said, *"Be not deceived; God is not mocked: for whatsoever a man soweth, that shall he also reap."* Basically, the idea here is whatever you put out there will eventually find you or come back to you. In Luke 6:37 we find, *"Judge not, and ye shall not be judged: condemn not, and ye shall*

Principles of Kingdom Living

not be condemned: forgive, and ye shall be forgiven." In this verse, three things are covered; judging, condemning, and forgiving. In all three, if we do what's right, the word tells us that right will come back to us. We accept the Bible as the Word of God and the truth of God; therefore, we believe what it says to us. Numbers 23:19 says, *"God is not a man that he should lie; neither the son of man, that he should repent: hath he said, and shall he not do it? Or hath he spoken, and shall he not make it good?"* When God says He's going to do something, He does it. So when He puts a principle in place, it happens just like He said it would. One principle we all experience everyday is that the sun comes up in the east and goes down in the west. If God can do that, what would make us think He couldn't make sure the other principles would work? The bottom line is that God's principles work, and if we want to see and experience the blessings from God, we've got to apply, **The Golden Rule!!**

Of all the verses of Scripture found in the Sermon on the Mount, this one verse is probably quoted and recited by Christians and non-Christians alike on a daily basis. *The Preacher's Outline and Sermon Bible* says of this verse, *"It is the summit of ethics, behavior, righteousness, and godliness. It is a very practical statement of God's love; that is, God has done to us just as He wants us to do to Him. God has treated us as He wants us to treat Him (and everyone else)."*[64] They go on to further say, *"The golden rule reveals the heart of God. It shows us exactly how God's heart longs for us to live and act. It is a simple statement revealing what love really is and what life in a perfect world is like....The golden rule is a one sentence statement that embraces all human behavior."*[65] Can you begin to imagine what our world and society would be like if we would all apply this simple yet profound principle on a daily basis?

Since this verse is called The Golden Rule, there must be other rules out there because gold is higher on the chart than other minerals. I'd like to share with you what some call The Silver Rules:

- The HINDU religion taught: *This is the sum of duty: do naught to others which if done to thee would cause thee pain.* - The Mahabharata

- The BUDDHIST religion taught: *Hurt not others with that which pains yourself.* - Udana-Varga

[64]Ibid, page 153
[65]Ibid, page 153

The Golden Rule

- The JEWISH traditions taught: *What is hateful to you, do not to your fellow men. That is the entire Law; all the rest is commentary.* - The Talmud

- The MUSLIM religion taught: *No one of you is a believer until he desires for his brother that which he desires for himself.* - Hadith

- The BAHA'I faith teaches: *He should not wish for others that which he doth not wish for himself, nor promise that which he doth not fulfil.* – The Book of Certitude[66]

Our responsibility as believers in Jesus Christ is to accept and follow the truths He has provided to us. I stated earlier that we accept the Word of God, or the Bible, as the truth of God, and therefore, that's what we apply to our lives. Our responsibility is applying **The Golden Rule!**

Concerning **The Golden Rule**...

This Applies to All Things in Our Lives

One of the key words in this verse is the word "all" which gives us direction from the Lord. Much like we don't have the right to pick and choose which part of the Bible we will or not follow, here Jesus makes it plain that this principle applies to all things in our lives. This would help us to understand that in our business dealings, in our personal dealings, in our church dealings, this principle applies. It's been said that, "if you want to be a leader, you must first be a follower!" Your ability to lead has a lot to do with how well you conducted yourself as a follower.

This Applies To All People In Our Lives

Just as it applies to all things, it also applies to all people in our lives. Let's be real–we have the tendency to write some people off, or we don't associate with some people because we feel we've been wronged by them, or they hurt our feelings in some way. We make it up in our minds that we will not have any further dealings with them because of that one or two incidents. If we are going to apply this rule as the Lord lays it out for us, that would mean it's applicable to those people also. Again, where would we be if the Lord wrote us off after one or two incidents?

[66] Anonymous

Principles of Kingdom Living

This Applies To All of Us

One thing about Jesus is that He did not come to destroy the Law, but to fulfill it! His last statement in this verse says, *"for this is the law and the prophets."* The Law shows us just how wretched we are, and the prophets point us to Jesus!!! Therefore, applying this rule to our lives enables us to get to that place of obedience with God, and draws us closer to Jesus our Savior! There are a lot of times in the church where people say that certain things don't apply to them. Not everybody will be the pastor; not everybody will be a preacher or deacon; not everybody will sing in the choir; not everybody will be part of the many ministries of the church, but every pastor, every preacher, every deacon, every choir member, and every member of the body of Christ has the responsibility to apply the Golden Rule to their lives. It's part of our obedience and submission to Christ, to live a life that's pleasing in His sight!

So in closing, when I think about John 3:16 which says, *"For God so loved the world, that he gave his only begotten Son, that whosoever believeth on him should not perish, but have everlasting life."* I can see The Golden Rule being applied by God Himself. He gave His Son's life for our sins, that we might give our lives to the Son and gain eternal life though Jesus. God promised that if we believed on the Son that we will have eternal life. I'm glad I know that God keeps all of His promises and His word tells us so. In 2 Peter 3:9 we find, *"The Lord is not slack concerning his promise, as some men count slackness; but is longsuffering to us-ward, not willing that any should perish, but that all should come to repentance."*

Jesus personified The Golden Rule by leaving heaven, coming down to earth, and living a sinless life as an example for us.

- While here He healed the sick, raised the dead, and gave sight to the blind.

- While here, He gave His life that we would have eternal life! He did so by dying on a cross on a hill called Calvary!

- He suffered so we wouldn't have to suffer. He endured the cross; He endured the grave; but early on Sunday morning, neither death nor the grave could hold my Jesus!!!

Principles of
KINGDOM LIVING
How to Live Right in a World Gone Wrong

CHAPTER
25

SALVATION IS A DECISION

"Enter ye in at the strait gate: for wide is the gate, and broad is the way, that leadeth to destruction, and many there be which go in thereat: Because strait is the gate, and narrow is the way, which leadeth unto life, and few there be that find it."

Matthew 7:13-14

Anybody who really knows me will tell you that I like options. The reason I like options is because I like to make informed decisions, especially about those things that will have a lasting effect or impact on my life. When I think about earthly decisions, I realize that I didn't buy the first car I saw; I didn't buy the first house I went into; I don't normally by the first suit I see; nor do I buy the first shirt or shoes I come across. I make sure whatever it is I'm buying, I have some kind of knowledge as to what it is, who made it, and if it's a major purchase, I make sure I get a warranty for the product!

Jesus is doing the same thing here in our text. He's making it plain as to the choices that are out there, and give some idea as to what to expect when the decision is made. If you really take a look at what Jesus is saying here, it's no different than what's been shared throughout the Scriptures. In Deuteronomy 30:19, God said, *"I call heaven and earth to record this day against you, that I have set before you life and death, blessing and cursing: therefore choose life, that both thou and thy seed may live."* Joshua made a decision for himself and tried to get the children of Israel to do the same. In Joshua 24:14-15, he said, *"Now therefore fear the Lord, and serve him in sincerity and in truth: and put away the gods which your fathers served on the other side of the flood, and in Egypt; and serve ye the Lord. 15 And if it seem evil unto you to serve the Lord, choose you this day whom ye will serve; whether the gods which your fathers served that were on the other side of the flood, or the gods of the Amorites, in whose land ye dwell: but as for me and my house, we will serve the Lord."*

Some people say and believe that there are many roads that lead to heaven, but the Bible tells us there's one way–His name is Jesus! When it comes to eternal life, **Salvation is a Decision!!!**

In this portion of the Sermon on the Mount, Jesus has just finished teaching on the Golden Rule, which is also a decision. It's a decision to do the right thing, or do what the world does and expect the consequences thereby. Now He's connecting that decision making process to the afterlife. Some people believe that once you die, that's it; or if you find yourself in hell, you will burn up instantly and it will be all over. Again, that's what the world thinks and in some cases believe, but I would encourage all of us to believe what Jesus tells us about the afterlife, and make a decision that will give us eternal Life!!!

In our text, Jesus talks about a strait gate and a wide gate. Let's look at what the text tells us.

There Are Two Gates[67]

One gate is called strait, and the other one is called wide. It's interesting that the text says many stand at the wide gate, and few at the straight

[67] Preacher's Outline and Sermon Bible, Matthew 1, Outline Only

gate. When you think about what the Bible says about salvation, you will find in Romans 3:23, *"For all have sinned and come short of the glory of God."* That sounds like all mankind is standing at the wide gate before a decision is made. That decision is found in John 3:16 at the end that says, *"for whosoever believeth on him should not perish, but have everlasting life."* Although Jesus died for the world, everybody is not going to accept Him, but everyone has a decision to make about the two gates. **Salvation is a Decision!**

There are Two Ways

The text says that there is a broad way and a narrow way regarding the gates. The broad and easy way has a reference to living without boundaries or no rules and regulations to follow. It's a no holds barred way of living. Many people live their lives like this because they don't like rules; they don't like structure; they don't like guidelines; but want to live life to the fullest. The problem with that is when you live like this, you live without purpose, and we're all here for a purpose! The narrow and hard way, as described by *The Preacher's Outline and Sermon Bible*, *"requires commitment, determination, discipline, control, and self-denial."* The narrow path requires you to stay alert, stay on task, stay on point, and stay focused. **Salvation is a Decision!!!**

There Are Two Ends

Since there are two gates, there must be two different destinations that they lead to. The text says the broad way leads to destruction, which can also be equated to death. Hebrews 9:27 says, *"And as it is appointed unto man once to die, but after this the judgment."* So we're all going to die one day, unless the rapture takes place first! The Bible not only talks about death, but also the second death as found in Revelation 21:8 which says, *"But the fearful, and unbelieving, and the abominable, and murderers, and whoremongers, and sorcerers, and idolaters, and all liars, shall have their part in the lake which burneth with fire and brimstone: which is the second death."* The broad gate leads to death and destruction, and it's interesting to note that the text says many will be there! Conversely, the narrow gate leads to life and not just life, but everlasting life! In John 10:10, Jesus said, *"…but I am come that you might have life, and of that more abundantly."* As believers in Christ, we are promised not just life, but abundant life, and it will only be received through Jesus Christ.

Principles of Kingdom Living

In John 14:6, He said, *"I am the way, the truth, and the life; no man cometh to the Father except by me."* **Salvation is a Decision!!!**

There are Two Decisions

The Preacher's Outline and Sermon Bible has a very interesting comment here. *"There are two decisions, no effort vs. seeking to find. The wide gate requires no decision to enter. A person stands before it automatically by being in the world. Christ does not say a person has to enter it. To enter the gate requires no energy, no search, no commitment. A person is there, facing the gate already. All he as to do is to begin his journey in life and follow it's broad and easy course. The narrow gate requires a decision to enter. It requires (1) a personal decision, (2) a firm decision, and (3) a commitment of energy and effort to search out the entrance. And once the narrow gate has been found, an immediate and definite decision to enter is required."*[68] There are times when we think that doing nothing is the best decision, but I would share that in this case, doing nothing is the worst decision. To do nothing will only lead to everlasting destruction, but a decision for Christ leads to everlasting life. Even when Jesus said in Matthew 11:28, *"Come unto me, all ye that labour and are heavy laden, and I will give you rest,"* that required a decision!

I can't speak for anybody, but as for me, as the songwriter said, "I have decided, to follow Jesus…no turning back…no turning back!" Why?

- He's the Alpha and the Omega, yet He made a decision to be born!
- He's the King of kings, and Lord of lords, yet He made a decision to become a ransom for many!
- He's Emmanuel, God with Us, yet he made a decision to leave heaven to save us!
- He's El-Elyon, the Almighty One, yet He made a decision to lay down His life for your sins and mine!

One of the reasons I'm following Jesus is because when they were walking Him up to Calvary, He didn't turn back! He went up to Calvary to be crucified on a cross, was placed in a borrowed tomb, and rose from the dead early on a Sunday morning!

---

[68]Ibid, Deeper Study #5, page 157

Principles of
KINGDOM LIVING
How to Live Right in a World Gone Wrong

CHAPTER
26

WATCH OUT FOR WOLVES!

"Beware of false prophets, which come to you in sheep's clothing, but inwardly they are ravening wolves. Ye shall know them by their fruits. Do men gather grapes of thorns, or figs of thistles? Even so every good tree bringeth forth good fruit; but a corrupt tree bringeth forth evil fruit. A good tree cannot bring forth evil fruit, neither can a corrupt tree bring forth good fruit. Every tree that bringeth not forth good fruit is hewn down, and cast into the fire. Wherefore by their fruits ye shall know them."

Matthew 7:15-20

Principles of Kingdom Living

It's been said that you can't judge a book by its cover. The cover can give you an idea as to what the book is about, but it can't tell you everything within. In order to know what's going on within the pages, you've got to make the time to read it, to see what the book is all about. In doing so, the mere words on the pages will reveal to you what the book is about, what it stands for, what it's opinions are, and how it will react or respond to certain situations.

In Bible days, God established prophets and teachers to teach and proclaim to the people His truths, and share with them the things that will come to pass in the days ahead. The way to know a real prophet from a false prophet was to see and know that what He said would come to pass. A true prophet of God would not tell people what he wanted to tell them, but would share with them what God has told him to share with them.

The Word of God warns us in Jeremiah 23:16, *"Thus saith the Lord of hosts, Hearken not unto the words of the prophets that prophesy unto you: they make you vain: they speak a vision of their own heart, and not out of the mouth of the Lord."*

Dr. Finis Dake says here, *"In detecting false spirits from the true, one should realize that any doctrine which denies, or in any way causes doubt and unbelief concerning anything taught in Scripture is demon inspired. Furthermore, any power, influence, or doctrine which causes one to become passive, inactive, submissive, and unresisting to all supernatural working seeking to control the life contrary to Scripture, is not of God."* [69]

In today's society, there are so many people who have appointed themselves to be prophets and teachers that it's important for us to be rooted and grounded in the truth of the Word of God. And in this day and age where everybody just wants a title, some people are proclaiming themselves to be prophets and teachers, all for the sake of their own personal gain. For example, today we have:

- Prosperity Prophets and Teachers: These are the ones who will tell you that if you contribute to their ministries, you will receive a blessing from God;

---

[69] Dake's Annotated Reference Bible, Dake's Bible Sales, Inc

- Healing Prophets and Teachers: These are the ones who will tell you that if you send them some money, they will send you back a special and anointed handkerchief or oil that will heal you of your sickness or disease;
- Opportunist Prophets and Teachers: These are the ones who pick a certain situation that most people are dealing with, i.e. the loss of job, home, etc., and tell you if you send them some money, in so many days, you will have what you lost, and then some!

Because of these false prophets:

There are people in our society who are broke, and still waiting for a blessing!

There are people in our society who are broke, and still waiting for their healing!

There are people in our society who are broke, and still waiting for the job or home they were promised!

The problem is that they put their faith and trust in the wrong person! It's because of that we have to **Watch Out For Wolves!!**

In this portion of the Sermon on the Mount, Jesus is telling His disciples to watch out for false prophets and teachers. Basically, He's telling them they look like the real thing, they act like the real thing, but they are not the real thing! I think it's important for us to understand that whatever God has established to be real, the devil also has his counterfeits, which trick and deceive people. The same can be said about prophets and teachers. The Lord starts out here with a warning.

There Will Be False Prophets (verse 15)

Just as there were false prophets then, there are false prophets today. The Apostle Paul spoke to this in Acts 20:29-30 when he said, *"For I know this, that after my departing shall grievous wolves enter in among you, not sparing the flock. Also of your own selves shall men arise, speaking perverse things, to draw away disciples after them."* You see, Paul knew that these false prophets would come to mislead people, and if you look carefully at what Paul was saying, he said that some of these prophets would come from within. It's interesting to me that churches don't normally fall apart over doctrine or teaching, but rather, over power and position. You see, we have to Watch Out for Wolves because just as the devil can appear as an angel of light, wolves in the house can appear to be workers of righteousness! When we remember that according to Isaiah 64:6, *"But we are all as an unclean thing, and all our righteousness are as filthy rags..."* anything and everything we do should reflect our relationship with Jesus because that's where our righteousness comes from. Again, Paul states the fact that in the latter times (and we're living in latter times), that false prophets will arise. He shares this in 1 Timothy 4:1 which reads, *"Now the Spirit speaketh expressly, that in the latter times some shall depart from the faith, giving heed to seducing spirits, and doctrine of devils."* Here he makes that case that people will flock to false prophets to hear what they want to hear, and not hear the truth. The reality of it all is that the truth will, (1) tell you about yourself; and (2), it has the power to set you free. Some people only want to hear those things that will justify their actions or deeds, instead of hearing the truth and being set free. Our society is full of false prophets, which is why we need to **Watch Out for Wolves!!!**

<u>There Are Ways To Identify Them (verse 16)</u>

In Matthew 7, we're told not to judge people, but here Jesus tells us that we can know what people are all about if we observe them over time. A lot of time, we're quick to make a judgment about somebody based on how they look, their ethnicity, or even how they dress, yet we don't know the real person under the clothes and skin. In identifying a false prophet, Jesus said we can know them by their fruit. Have you ever heard the statement, "the fruit doesn't fall far from the tree?" Here we have the same principle because the fruit of false prophets will be just like them. Have you ever come across somebody who is just messy, or likes to keep up drama all the time? You see how they are, and then low and behold, the people they associate with start acting just like them! The same applies to false prophets who are teaching "another gospel" and their followers become just like them. They use deceptive words and twist the Scriptures to support their message, much like Satan did with Jesus in the wilderness.

Watch Out For Wolves!

In 2 Timothy 3:13, Paul said, *"But evil men and seducers shall wax worse and worse, deceiving, and being deceived."* They spend their time deceiving people and over time people don't know they are being deceived. The main way to know they are false prophets is to know the truth! When you know the truth, it's hard to fall prey to false prophets.

So if we want to identify false prophets, we must know the truth. Jesus was praying to the Father one day and said in John 17:17, *"Sanctify them through thy truth, thy word is truth."* He also said that it's the truth that will make us free. In John 8:32, Jesus Himself said, *"And ye shall know the truth, and the truth shall make you free."* So I guess the question at hand is, what or who is the truth? I'm glad you asked and that answer is found in John 14:6 when Jesus said, *"I am the way, the truth, and the life: no man cometh unto the father except by me."*

- If they are preaching another Jesus–they are a false prophet;
- If they are preaching there are many ways to eternal life–they are a false prophet;
- If their doctrine centers around them and not the saving power of Jesus–they are a false prophet;
- If they teach anything contrary to what Jesus taught–they are a false prophet;
- If they teach the Bible is based on your own private interpretation–they are a false prophet!

Here's truth!

Jesus came down through 42 generations to save a wretch like me!

Jesus was born of a virgin named Mary to become a ransom for many!

Jesus endured persecution and hardships so that we can have a right to eternal life!

Jesus hung, bled, and died on Calvary's cross to pay for the sins of this world!

Jesus was buried in a borrowed tomb to prove He died on the cross!

Principles of Kingdom Living

Jesus rose early on a Sunday morning with all power in His hands!

Jesus ascended into heaven and is now seated on the right hand of the Father!

Jesus is coming back again one day! Will you be ready when He comes?

Watch Out for Wolves, but know that Jesus is the Truth!!!

Principles of
KINGDOM LIVING
How to Live Right in a World Gone Wrong

CHAPTER 27

PART-TIME MEMBERS IN A FULL-TIME CHURCH!

"Not every one that saith unto me, Lord, Lord, shall enter into the Kingdom of Heaven; but he that doeth the will of my Father which is in heaven. Many will say to me in that day, Lord, Lord, have we not prophesied in thy name? and in thy name have cast out devils? and in thy name done many wonderful works? And then will I profess unto them, I never knew you: depart from me, ye that work iniquity."

Matthew 7:21-23

In the job market today, you have part-time workers and full-time workers; and the primary differences between the two are the hours worked each week and the benefits they receive. It's understood up from that the difference exists, but sometimes the part-time worker wants the same benefits and entitlements as the full-time worker. They figure since they wear the same uniform, work in the same environment, and get paid by the same employer, they can have the same benefits too. The problem with this is the agreement entered into at the very beginning. It reminds me of a Biblical story (in reverse) of the master who had a vineyard and had people working for him. He had some who started at the beginning of the day, mid-day, and then at the end of the day. When the day was over, he paid each worker a penny as promised, but the folks who worked the longest felt that they should be paid more because of how long they worked. He told them what the initial agreement was and paid them accordingly.

It's interesting to me that this same mentality is in the church because generally speaking, members want all the benefits without doing everything that's necessary to achieve them. For example, social security did not start out as a retirement plan, but you can't draw from it in your latter years unless you put something into it. The same applies to a pension plan, an IRA, 401(k), and so on.

The church of Jesus Christ is not a part-time assignment, but a full-time requirement! In Luke 19, Jesus gives an account of a master who went to get a kingdom, but before he left, he called 10 of his servants to him, gave them 10 pounds (money) each, and told them to *"occupy till I come."*[70] In other words, he gave them what they needed and told them to keep doing business until he returned. Jesus has done the same thing with us in that He's given us the Word of God and the Spirit of God to proclaim the Living God, but we can't be **Part-Time Members in a Full-Time Church!**

This part of the Sermon on the Mount deals with people professing to have a relationship with Christ, and the fact that there's no real evidence to support it. Some would say they are "perpetrating a fraud" by looking the part, but not living it! Jesus makes it very plain what will happen to those who are living to impress people instead of living to be obedient to Him. Let's see what we have in the text about **Part-Time Members in a Full-Time Church.**

Three things about Part-Time Members:

[70]Luke 19:13

Part-Time Members In A Full-Time Church!

They Won't Do What's Required (verse 21)

As a member of the church, at least a couple of things are required.

First, we're required to be in regular attendance when worship takes place. Hebrews 10:25 says, *"Not forsaking the assembling of ourselves together, as the manner of some is; but exhorting one another, and so much the more: as you see the day approaching."* You see, a part-time member will attend worship on the days in which it's convenient for them, when it doesn't interfere with their schedule. They attend on the first and third Sundays because they've got other things planned on the other Sundays. They don't attend Sunday School, weekly ministry meetings, or Bible Study because that's what full-time members do.

Second, they don't give Biblically, but will be the first one to say, "…but God knows my heart." They want a full-time blessing; they want a full-time healing; they want a full-time breakthrough, yet want to give a part-time offering to God. Through the prophet Malachi, God said in Malachi 3:10 to *"Bring ye all the tithes into the storehouse, that there may be meat in mine house…"* A part-time member will bring part of the tithe, but anticipates full blessings from God! However, when we meet the requirement, we're fulfilling the will of God and doing those things that pleases Him. *The Preacher's Outline and Sermon Bible* says, *"A person must do God's will in order to enter heaven. Note: Christ is talking about people who are interested in heaven. He is not talking about those who are not interested in heaven. Heaven should be the final goal of every man. It should be the place every man seeks to enter."* God has so many blessings for us and all He wants is for us to meet the condition. But part-time members won't do what's required!!

They Talk A Good Game (verse 22)

What I saw in this verse is a part-time member talking the talk, but not walking the walk. They look like a full-time member, but if you watch them long enough, they don't exhibit full-time attributes. They know all the "Christianese," they say all the right things at the right time, yet it's empty because there's no relationship with Jesus as their foundation. They're quick to say, "bless the Lord, O my soul, and all that is within

Principles of Kingdom Living

me; bless His holy name" or they will say something like, "giving honor to God who is the head of my life," and five minutes later will cut their eyes at somebody because they looked at them funny! They may even go to work or talk with their neighbors and tell them, "see, I'm a good Christian because I go to church sometimes and I made a donation to Father Joe's Village!" Jesus tells us they will say things like, *"have we not prophesied in thy name? and in thy name have cast out devils?"* The Apostle Paul speaks to this in Romans 10:3 where it says, *"For they being ignorant of God's righteousness, and going about to establish their own righteousness, have not submitted themselves unto the righteousness of God."* There's more to it than to give the Lord lip service – He's looking for full-time service. They Talk A Good Game!!

They're Gonna Get Their Feelings Hurt! (verse 23)

Again, *The Preacher's Outline and Sermon Bible* says, *"Christ never knew the false professors – not personally. False professors do not know Christ personally; they do not acknowledge His redemption and their need for His redemption. They never come to Him for personal salvation. Therefore, Christ never has the chance to know them. In the Day of Judgment He is tragically forced to pronounce the truth: "I never knew you."* [71] It will be a shame and a tragedy when people are standing at the Great White Throne Judgment, having spent their entire lives with their names on the church rolls, but their names are not found in the Lamb's Book of Life! They've spent their lives talking negatively about the pastor, discounting the deacons, being uncooperative with the ushers because they want to sit where they want to sit, complaining about the choir, manipulating other members, short changing God in their giving, and now God is getting the last word! When Jesus came here from heaven, He said in Matthew 11:28, *"Come unto me all ye that labour and are heavy laden, and I will give you rest,"* yet now in heaven He's saying *"depart from me ye worker of iniquity!"* In the original Greek, the word depart means to go away, or be separated. Eternal damnation means to be separated from Jesus eternally. You see, you can't expect full-time benefits by only giving part-time service.

We know that naturally there are benefits having worked your entire adult life and retiring. In most cases, you'll receive a pension, or you'll be able to

---

[71] Preacher's Outline and Sermon Bible, Matthew 1, page 166

Part-Time Members In A Full-Time Church!

take advantage of your savings and investments, thus enabling you to live a worry and stress free life financially in retirement.

Just like in retirement, there is no more work, heaven is also a land of no more:

- No more pain;
- No more suffering;
- No more sickness;
- No more disease;
- No more high blood pressure;
- No more diabetes;
- No more arthritis;
- No more cancer;
- No more stress;
- No more drama!

But you will find 12 gates to the city and streets paved with gold;

On both sides of the streets will be the tree of life, giving off 12 manner of fruit, one for each month of the year, and the leaves will be for the healing of the nations.

But the best part about it is that Jesus Himself will be there! Do you know who Jesus is?

When He comes back, will you be a part-time member in a full-time church, or a faithful full-time member in a full-time church?

Principles of
KINGDOM LIVING
How to Live Right in a World Gone Wrong

CHAPTER

28

HOW'S YOUR FOUNDATION?

"Therefore whosoever heareth these sayings of mine, and doeth them, I will liken him unto a wise man, which built his house upon a rock: And the rain descended, and the floods came, and the winds blew, and beat upon that house; and it fell not: for it was founded upon a rock. And every one that heareth these sayings of mine, and doeth them not, shall be likened unto a foolish man, which built his house upon the sand: And the rain descended, and the floods came, and the winds blew, and beat upon that house; and it fell: and great was the fall of it. And it came to pass, when Jesus had ended these sayings, the people were astonished

Principles of Kingdom Living

at his doctrine: For he taught them as one having authority, and not as the scribes."

Matthew 7:24-29

If you want something to stand throughout the test of time and chance, it needs to have a firm foundation. It's been said that if you want to construct a very tall building going up, you must dig deeper for the foundation. For the most part, you have to dig down about 2-3 feet in order to establish a firm foundation for a house; but for a skyscraper, you've got to go down a whole lot deeper.

The foundation is necessary as it keeps the building grounded and stabilizes it during rough times. Nature is so strong that it has the ability to take a house off its foundation and throw it in some cases, yards or miles away. The right foundation can keep a house intact even during the toughest of storms.

Your spiritual foundation determines just how much you will be thrown around during tough times. If you work on your Spiritual Growth and development, no matter what comes your way, you know that with you and the Lord, you can handle it. If you don't work on your Spiritual Growth, then when trials and tribulations show up – and they will - you tend to wonder how you're going to make it. The Apostle Paul encourages us in Ephesians 4:14, *"That we henceforth be no more children, tossed to and fro, and carried about by the sleight of men, and cunning craftiness, whereby they lie in wait to deceive."* Please be mindful that because you are a child of God, the devil has a target on you, wants to deceive you, and take you off your foundation, if you let him. The only power he has is the power we give him, so we need to have a firm or sure foundation. Concerning the devil, the Bible teaches us in 1 Peter 5:8 to *"Be sober, be vigilant; because your adversary the devil, as a roaring lion, walketh about, seeking whom he may devour."* This would tell us that as one who wants to devour us, he also wants to take us off our foundation and cause havoc and destruction to enter into our lives.

If you have the right foundation, you don't have to worry about trials, tribulations, or storms to come into your life, because you have a firm

How's Your Foundation?

foundation to withstand those things. I would submit to you that having Jesus Christ as your foundation will give you exactly what you need to endure the storms of life. So the question before us today is–**How's Your Foundation?**

Our Lord has made His way down to the end of His Sermon on the Mount and it's interesting that He's talking about foundations now. He's dealt with a myriad of issues throughout this sermon and now He sums it up around having a good foundation. If you make a close examination of the text, you will find that in order to have a good or solid foundation something is required – hearing and doing what He says! Let's be mindful that obedience goes a long way with the Lord and He always blesses obedience. We're told in 1 Peter 1:22 to, *"Be ye doers of the word, and not hearers only, deceiving your own selves."* It's one thing to hear it, but it's another thing entirely to do it! One thing I've discovered is that people hear what they want to hear! If it's something that interests them, they will hear clearly what's being said. But if it's something they are not interested in, they will nonchalantly hear it, but not take action on it. Trust me when I tell you that Jesus is not speaking nonchalantly to us, but directly and purposefully, so that we can be the beneficiaries of His words and blessings!! So let's examine just what the Lord is saying here!

There are a couple of questions I need to ask.

Are You A Wise Builder? (verses 24-25)

Notice if you will what the wise builder does. (1) He hears what Jesus is saying and, (2) he builds on that. One of the things that distinguishes him as a wise builder is the fact that he hears and obeys! How many times have we seen people hear what's being told to them, only to find out they didn't apply what they heard? They hear the preacher say to, *"Trust in the Lord with all thine heart..."*[72] yet when things go awry, they immediately rely on their own knowledge and understanding, only to find out it's not working for them. King Solomon said in Proverbs 1:5, *"A wise man will hear, and will increase learning; and a man of understanding shall attain unto wise counsel."* He also said in Proverbs 8:33 to, *"Hear instruction and be wise, and refuse it not."* A wise builder realizes that he does not know it all and needs to hear from someone who will give him solid information

---

[72]Proverbs 3:5

and direction. Here in the text, Jesus says that the one who hears what He says and does it, He will liken them unto a wise man.

- When you hear truth, it would behoove you to heed it;
- When you hear truth; it would be in your best interest to do what it says;
- When you hear truth, it has the power to set you free!!

The person who hears truth knows that it has the power to hold them up, keep them, sustain them, and even bring them out in times of trouble. The reason for that is the foundation that truth lays for the believer! Having lived in my house for a long time, I'm very confident about the foundation the house is on. I'm even more confident about my spiritual foundation because I know it's Jesus!!! The text says that the wise man builds his house on a rock because it's solid, steadfast, and unmovable! When your foundation is the Lord, here's what the Bible says in:

- Psalm 18:2, *"The Lord is my rock, and my fortress, and my deliverer; my God, my strength, in whom I will trust; my buckler, and the horn of my salvation, and my high tower."*
- Psalm 62:2, *"He only is my rock and my salvation; he is my defence; I shall not be greatly moved."*
- Psalm 94:22, *"But the Lord is my defence; and my God is the rock of my refuge."*

The question is–**How Is Your Foundation?**

The last question before us is:

Are You A Foolish Builder? (verses 26-27)

Believe it or not, the word, "foolish", from the original Greek actually means dull or stupid, heedless; blockhead! Do you remember watching the Charlie Brown cartoons back in the day, and Lucy would always call Charlie Brown a blockhead? She did so because she thought he did things in a dumb or stupid way, so that's what she called him. Isn't it

How's Your Foundation?

interesting that the Greek definition for the word foolish means the same thing?

What caught my eye here is that both the wise and foolish men had the opportunity to hear what Jesus was saying, but only one of them acted on it. The foolish man made a choice not to do what the Lord said and consequently paid the price for it. If I can be real here, this same thing happens today in our society and we sometimes wonder why things are working out the way they are. The foolish builder was concerned about today and not tomorrow and that's a dangerous place to be. Too many people today are doing that. They buy the latest fashions and the latest gadgets, but don't have any money set aside for retirement, or a rainy day; they have cellphones, but don't have savings accounts; they've made it up in their minds that when it's time for them to go, it's somebody else's responsibility to bury them. I don't know about you, but that is foolishness!!!

Jesus said that because the foolish man built his house on the sand, the storm came and the house fell!! Dr. Albert Barnes said, *"The house built on the sand is beat upon by the floods and rains; it's foundation gradually is worn away; it falls, and is borne down the stream and destroyed. So falls the sinner."*[73] If you noticed what Dr. Barnes said, the destruction can be a gradual thing and happen over time. When we know the devil's mission statement as found in John 10:10 where it says, *"The thief cometh not, but for to steal, and for to kill, and to destroy..."* NEWSFLASH!!! The devil is not concerned about destroying you immediately; he's more concerned about destroying you completely. If he can't do it right now, he'll work at doing it over time! The last thing we need to do is help him to destroy us! The Prophet Jeremiah said in Jeremiah 17:5, *"Thus saith the Lord, Cursed be the man that trusteth in man, and maketh flesh his arm, and whose heart departeth from the Lord."* When we make it a point to put our complete trust in ourselves and not in the Lord, we become the foolish builder and the things around us will begin falling apart!

So the question before us is, How's Your Foundation? If you find yourself sinking in sand, or your foundation is being hit by the storms

---

[73] Dr. Albert Barnes, "Barnes' Notes of the Gospel of Matthew"

Principles of Kingdom Living

of life, it's not too late to get a good foundation! I would recommend you give the Rock a chance to stabilize you, whose name is Jesus! The Bible says in:

- Deuteronomy 32:4, *"He is the Rock, his work is perfect: for all his ways are judgment: a God of truth and without iniquity, just and right is he."*
- Psalm 94:22, *"But the Lord is my defence; and my God is the rock of my refuge."*
- 1 Corinthians 10:4, *"And did all drink the same spiritual drink; for they drank of that spiritual Rock that followed them: and that Rock was Christ."*

If you're not sure who I'm talking about, His name is Jesus Christ and He's in the miracle working business:

- He was born of a virgin; that was a miracle;
- He cleansed lepers; that was a miracle!
- He healed Peter's mother-in-law; that was a miracle!
- He healed or delivered a demon possessed man in the cemetery; that was miracle!
- He healed a paralyzed man; that was a miracle!
- He healed a man with a withered hand; that was a miracle!
- He healed the centurion's servant; that was a miracle!
- He raised a widow's son from the dead; that was a miracle!
- He spoke to the wind and the waves and they obeyed Him; that was a miracle!
- He healed a woman who had an issue of blood; that was a miracle!
- He fed 5000 men with two fish and five barley loaves of bread; that was a miracle!
- He endured the beatings of the Roman soldiers; that was a miracle!

How's Your Foundation?

- He hung, bled, and died for your sins and mine; that was a miracle!
- He was resurrected on a Sunday morning with all power in His hands; that was a miracle!
- He ascended into heaven on a cloud; that was a miracle!

Since we know He's done all those things; we can also know He can be the Rock we need to stabilize us!

Get rid of that sand and get yourself a Rock named Jesus!!

How's Your Foundation?

Principles of Kingdom Living

BIBLIOGRAPHY

American Heritage Dictionary, Third Edition, Houghton Mifflin Publishers

Amplified Bible, © 1965, Zondervan Publishing House, Grand Rapids, MI

Barnes, Albert, "Barnes' Notes of the New Testament," Baker House Books, Grand Rapids, MI

Dake, Finis J, "Dake's Annotated Reference Bible," Dake Bible Sales, Inc, Lawrenceville, GA

Dictionary.com, Internet

Henry, Matthew, "Matthew Henry's Commentary," Volume 5, Matthew to John, Hendrickson Publishers

Lockyer, Herbert, "All the Men of the Bible," Zondervan Books, Zondervan Publishing House, Grand Rapids, MI

"All the Promises of the Bible," Zondervan Books, Zondervan Publishing House, Grand Rapids, MI

Preachers Outline and Sermon Bible, The Gospel of Matthew, Volume 1, Leadership Ministries Worldwide

Pulpit Commentary, Matthew, Volume VX, H. D. M. Spence and Joseph S. Exell, Editors, Hendrickson Publishers

Strong, Edward, "Strong's Exhaustive Concordance of the Bible," Updated Edition, Hendrickson Publishers

Unger, Merrill F., The New Unger's Bible Dictionary, Moody Press, Chicago

www.godwithyou.org/charles-spurgeon-quotes/charles-spurgeon-quotes-on-prayer.htm, Internet

NOTES:

NOTES:

NOTES:

NOTES:

NOTES: